A PACK SCOUTER'S ACTIVITY BOOK

A PACK SCOUTER'S ACTIVITY BOOK

By

JEAN BARROW

Publication approved by The Scout Association, London

GLASGOW
BROWN, SON & FERGUSON, LIMITED
52 DARNLEY STREET

First Edition - 1975
Revised - - 1976
Second Edition - 1978
Revised - - 1981

ISBN 0 85174 415 X
ISBN 0 85174 334 X (SECOND EDITION)
ISBN 0 85174 265 3 (REVISED FIRST EDITION)

Printed and Made in Great Britain

INTRODUCTION

I HOPE you will find this book a help when planning your programmes. I have run both town and rural Packs, and know from experience that a programme which works with one Pack does not necessarily work with another. So much depends on the boy, the meeting place and what facilities are available. Therefore, may I suggest that when you read this book for ideas, you perhaps alter or adjust to suit your particular Pack.

CONTENTS

PROGRAMME PLANNING

How many of us sit and sigh over our programmes, longing for inspiration and leafing through our games-books, knowing that tomorrow is Pack Night again?

Remember, that first of all a boy looks for fun when he joins our Pack, and this means planning well, making all our activities instructive as well as full of fun, and most of all this means **planning ahead.**

An outline plan for the Seasons is ideal—January to March, April to July, (August—holiday activities or camp) and September to December. This would also give all who are running the programmes plenty of time for preparation. It is no good deciding on simple handcraft only a day or two before your Meeting. Also planning well ahead not only ensures that we have balanced programmes, but gives us plenty of time to find the expert for our many activities.

First of all decide on your monthly themes, suitable for the months; then make a list of special days (i.e. Saint's days, Hallowe'en, Shrove Tuesday, etc.), District events, Job Week, National events, etc. An outline plan is all that is needed at this stage, because as the weeks progress, there are bound to be alterations and additions. Next plan in detail one month's programmes, making sure that there is an even follow-through each week. Always be prepared to scrap something at the last minute, maybe because of weather, Cubs' mood or time. It is just as important to finish your Meetings on time as it is to start on time.

Let the parents in on future plans well ahead, and you will always get full co-operation from them.

Try and make your outings fit into your monthly theme. A visit to the Zoo to correspond with the Animal Lover Badge, the Planetarium to fit in with an Arrow activity on stars, a Weather Station or a visit to an inshore lighthouse if you are having weather as your theme, and so on.

The Arrows and Badges give us an excellent chance to introduce all sorts of exciting projects and activities into our meetings. Many Scouters may say what's the point of trying any of these activities when the boys are doing most of them in schools today. Admittedly the schools have changed their way of teaching, so that it is now on the lines of what most Scouters have been doing in their Packs for years.

This is where Teacher/Scouter co-operation is needed. Yes, I know many of you will be saying that teachers are not prepared to co-operate with what they consider are lay people, but where they do repetition is often avoided, a different approach to a project can be tried, and in many cases a more detailed follow-up can be done on Pack Nights. Teachers know well in advance of the next school year what radio and television programmes the children will be watching and working on, so if you are on friendly terms with the teachers of the school most of your Cubs go to, this should be a great help when doing your outline planning. Ask the school what Educational Visits are planned and so avoid repetition.

Ideas for programmes and activities can be found almost anywhere. Newspapers are a wonderful source for yarns, also the boys' weekly magazine, *Look and Learn*. These have excellent colour pictures that can either be made into wall charts or used for flip charts or even put into scrapbooks. Women's magazines help in all sorts of ways. Around Christmas time they are full of ideas for decorations, presents and handicraft. If these are all cut out and placed in a folder, you are bound to want to refer to them time and time again.

The *Woman* magazine has a free leaflet called 'Visitors Welcome'; also a leaflet on 'Bulk Buying and fund raising ideas'. Even a gardening magazine would hold ideas for a meeting.

The Child Education Quarterly, published by Evans has given articles on bird migration, weather and cloud formations, space projects and stories, all of which can be used in your activities.

Junior Education is a monthly magazine. This would put the Scouter right into the picture on day-to-day happenings in our schools. There are also useful projects, new ideas, etc., that can be adapted to suit your needs. New books are reviewed monthly.

Art and Craft in Education, published monthly by Evans, has a store of art and craft ideas which can be used in your Pack. Readers are informed about the latest craft books, and new mediums are discussed and ideas given for their use.

A wonderful book which Cubs really love is *The Incredible Adventures of Professor Branestawm*, by Norman Hunter and published by Puffin. Read just one adventure to your boys, and you will find them clamouring for the following 13 stories. There are even 76 Heath Robinson illustrations with which to delight everyone, and if you are clever enough to copy these drawings on to large sheets of stiff paper, do so, because Cubs love to pour over these after each story. A further 14 stories of this eccentric genius can be found in *Professor Branestawm's Treasure Hunt*.

The many Ladybird Books give ideas for programmes and special activities. The four Junior Science books will help with the three experiments in the 'Discovering' section; the *Learnabout* series, the *Recognition* series and the *Achievements* book series all cover many Arrow activities in all the sections.

Write for a free illustrated list from the Publishers—LADYBIRD BOOKS LTD., Loughborough, Leicestershire.

SCOUTING. The Scout Association's own monthly magazine is an invaluable aid to programme planning and for up-to-the-minute information. A free copy is available on request from Baden-Powell House.

Lego. Many Cubs collect Lego. These small bricks are ideal for constructing a working model, such as a drawbridge, conveyor belt, a windmill, etc. (Discovering.)

Write to LEGO LTD., Wrexham, Clwyd, LL13 9UH for their latest leaflet.

Communication (*Thinking*). For those of you who find yourself rather rusty at semaphore or morse, BROWN, SON & FERGUSON, LTD., 52 Darnley Street, Glasgow G41 2SG, have packs of cards with either morse or semaphore on one side, and the meanings on the reverse. These packs of cards are very popular as a quick and easy way of learning to signal.

Spring

ST. VALENTINE'S DAY.

(*a*) Make this a Special Pack Meeting, and send out invitation cards (made by the Cubs) to the Brownies and Brownie Guiders. It might be best for Scouters and Guiders to get together and plan the evening. A good finish would be a camp fire, hot cocoa and biscuits.

(*b*) How about the Cubs making a St. Valentine Card for their Mothers? They will enjoy making them, and their Mothers will no doubt be very thrilled.

MOTHERING SUNDAY.

(*a*) On the Pack Meeting before Mothering Sunday, let the boys make a card to give to their Mothers. Before the Meeting, Scouters will need to hunt out old greetings cards, gardening catalogues, magazines and coloured postcards. Provide each boy with a folded piece of paper, 5 in. × 4 in., and each Six with a pot of glue, then let them make their own

card. Perhaps Akela could write out one or two sample verses for the boys to copy, if they cannot think up one for themselves.

Another idea for an attractive card would be to draw a large butterfly or bird on the front of the card, and stick on pieces of different coloured chocolate wrappers.

(*b*) **Paper Doyley for Mother.**

Give each Cub a sheet of coloured paper and show them how to fold it in half, half again and yet again, and then tear out tiny pieces here and there. Finally open it out to find what sort of pattern has been made. If these are stuck on to coloured card, they would make rather attractive place settings.

EASTER BONNETS.

One evening near Easter, tell your Cubs about the custom of women buying an Easter Bonnet, and how you, too, wish to have one. Tell them they are now the great Paris hat designers,

and that you and Baloo would like to take advantage of this and have a hat designed by them for this Easter. Give the Cubs pieces of crêpe paper of various colours, pins, wool and cardboard, etc., and ask for two designs per Six. These should be modelled on Cubs who parade round your headquarters for the Scouters to make their choice before trying on the winning model. If you have the record of the film *Easter Parade* this could be played whilst the boys parade in their circle.

SCOUT JOB WEEK.

Cub Scouts are usually very enthusiastic about taking part in the annual Scout Job Week, but some encouragement and help is needed for the younger boy who is rather shy of setting out on his first year of jobs. It is, therefore, a wise Akela who uses Scout Job Week as his theme for several weeks before Easter.

(*a*) Scouters act the part of the public, and each Six takes it in turn to come up and knock at the door to ask for a job. Points to be given on politeness, smartness, efficiency of job given, and giving the correct answers. Scouters could be (*a*) lady who has never heard of Scout Job Week and asks a lot of questions; (*b*) man who expects boys to do a difficult or dangerous job; (*c*) lady who does not know what sort of jobs they can do, etc.

(*b*) All the Cubs will want to take a poster home to display in their window or other prominent place, but this can work out expensive for the whole Pack. Why not hold a competition for the best Job Week poster designed and painted by the boys. Perhaps the best could be displayed in the window of the local Post Office or store.

(*c*) Read a yarn to the boys using Job Week as the theme.

(*d*) Encourage the older Cubs to tell the Pack about some of their jobs from last year.

OXFORD VERSUS CAMBRIDGE.

On the Pack Meeting nearest this Boat Race, have the Pack divided in two for the evening. Scouters or Cubs could make large royal and sky-blue rosettes of crêpe paper to pin on to their uniform. There are many suitable games to be found in any games book. For example—ROWING RELAY. Cubs sit. Sixer as Cox faces the rest of the Six who are crew and hold on to the shoulders of the boy in front. Akela calls a number from 1–10, and under the Cox's direction, the crew row the correct number of strokes, then get up and run and form up at the other end of the room.

PARENTS' EVENINGS.

One of the most popular forms of Parents' Evening is to have the first half consisting of games, with a few games for Cubs only, and then Cubs versus Mothers and Cubs versus Fathers. This is followed by a short break when Cubs serve their parents with tea and cakes; then after a quick rearrangement of chairs, there comes the second half of the evening with some entertainment by the Cubs.

GAMES FOR CUBS VERSUS FATHERS.

(*a*) **Handyman Relay.**

Equipment needed: needle, cotton, patch } per Six

Ask for one volunteer from each Six to lie face-down on the floor at the far end of the hall. Place a patch on each of these boys' trousers. Give No. 1 a needle and cotton, and on the word 'Go', he runs up and starts sewing on patch. When the whistle blows, No. 1 runs back and touches off No. 2, who carries on stitching, and so on. Points deducted for any pricking with needle!

(*b*) **Tying a tie relay.**

Equipment needed: one tie per Six

Boys and fathers run up in relay formation, pick up a tie, which is hung over the back of a chair and tie it in the correct fashion round their necks. When it has been checked by Akela, tie is undone and boy or father runs back to touch off the next member of his Six.

(*c*) **Tug-of-War. Thread the Needle.**

Equipment needed: one thick rope
two thinner ropes

Two teams facing each other and numbered from opposite ends. In the middle is a thick rope and at each end of the room stands a Scouter or Cub Instructor with a loop of the thinner rope. The teams are told which end of the thick rope they are to pick up and into which loop they are to thread it when their number is called.

GAMES FOR CUBS VERSUS MOTHERS.

(*a*) **Book Balancing Relay.**

Equipment needed: one book per Six

Book is balanced on head. Cub kneels at the halfway mark and then continues the course.

(*b*) **Thread the Needle Relay.**

Equipment needed: one needle per Six
one piece of cotton per
boy or mother

Place the needle and a piece of cotton on a chair in front of each Six some distance away. Give the Cubs a needle with a bigger eye than the one the mothers have.

(*c*) **Pegging-out the Nappies.**

Equipment needed: one kitchen roll
one washing line
two pegs per boy or mother

Cubs and mothers in relay formation run up to the line and peg-up one nappy (piece of kitchen roll) each. First Six to finish and standing in a straight line is the winner. On the call 'It's raining', each boy and mother runs up in turn, unpegs 'nappy' and runs back to Six.

. . . . .

Let the games the Cubs play on their own demonstrate the Arrow and Proficiency Badge requirements.

999 CALL.

(*a*) How about a visit to your local Fire Station? The Cubs will be thrilled with everything, and the appliances and pole will be an enormous attraction. They might even be lucky enough to be there when a call comes in.

(*b*) The older Cubs would be interested in seeing what goes on behind the scenes in your local Telephone Exchange.

PENCILS.

Cubs rarely seem to have pencils, or else they carry around a small stub, usually without a point, buried somewhere in their pockets amongst a wonderful collection of odds and ends. Ask your boys to carry a pencil in their right sock and hold surprise inspections now and again. This will, without doubt, appeal to your Cubs, and there will be no more pencil hunting and holding up games.

COLLECTION.

Whilst on the subject of little boys' pockets and all the treasures they contain, ask the Cubs in their Sixes to empty out their pockets. Give points for the most useful collection, the most unusual collection, etc.

SPECIAL SERVICE.

So many Scout Groups and other Voluntary Organisations concentrate a lot of effort on a special service around Christmas-time, and the Children's Homes and old people get forgotten for the rest of the year.

Perhaps you could invite a group of children from a local Home to join you on a Cub picnic party, or give each Cub one potato to plant in a corner of his garden, then hold a competition to see whose plant yields the greatest weight of potatoes. These potatoes could then be put into bags and distributed to local senior citizens.

A GARDEN MAP OF BIRDS (Animal Lover Badge).

An interesting activity would be for each boy to draw out a plan of his garden on a sheet of paper that will stick nicely into his Cub scrapbook. Tell the Cubs to make observations of their garden before and after school each day, and to mark down on their map which birds visit their garden, exactly what part of it each bird favours, any nest-building and so on.

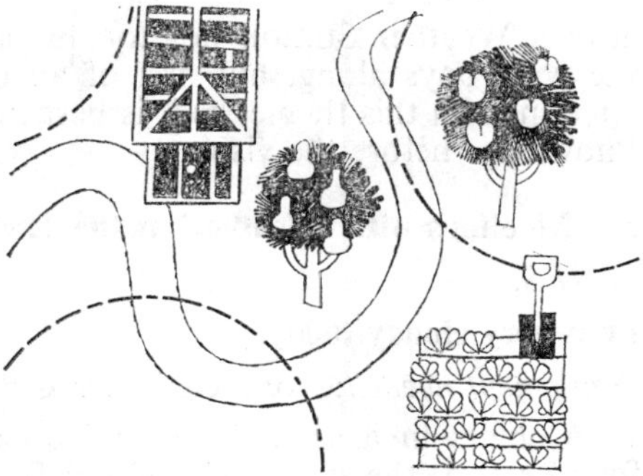

PACK PROJECT FOR COUNTRY CUBS (Handyman Badge).

Get help from parents or friends, and spend one or two Pack Meetings making bird nest-boxes, or bird tables. If you decide on the former, let each Cub choose which bird he will make a box for. There are many good books to help

you, but one that has much to recommend it is:
The Bird Table Book, by Tony Soper (Pan Books Ltd.). This book covers far more than its title suggests, and is packed with fascinating information.

WEATHER—March.

If you have a Weather Station not too far away, ask if you may take your boys along, but first of all hold two or three Pack Meetings on this theme, as it is best that the Cubs have some knowledge before the visit.

Ideas for Pack Meetings with 'Weather' as the Theme.

CLOUD GAMES.

(*a*) **'The sky is very cloudy today.'**

Equipment needed: one chair per Cub

Cubs sit on chairs in a semi-circle. Give each Cub, in groups of four or five, the name of a cloud formation, i.e. Cumulus, Cirrus, Stratus, Alto Cumulus, Cumulo-Nimbus.

When Akela calls out a certain cloud, those boys run through the opening and round the back of the chairs in a clockwise direction. (It will help if a short description follows each cloud name, i.e. Cumulus, the cauliflower cloud; Cirrus, thin and wispy, and so on). When 'The sky is very cloudy today' is called, every Cub gets up and runs round the chairs.

When 'The sun shines' is called, all 'clouds' continue running until each reaches opening and then scurries inside and on to a chair. In the meantime, one chair has been turned round, so in the case of a small Pack one boy is out and sits on that chair for the rest of the game. In a larger Pack, it is better for the boy who is forced to take the turned chair to lose a point for his Six.

(*b*) **Cloud Pictures.**

Equipment needed: pictures, postcards and even drawings of different cloud formations

Cubs in Sixes are numbered. Several yards in front are scattered postcards, etc., showing easily recognisable clouds.

Akela calls cloud and number. The Cub with that number runs up, selects which card he thinks is correct and runs with it to Akela. If the card is correct, the Cub runs and puts it back with the others and races back to his Six.

(*c*) **Cloud Run.**

Equipment needed: none

Cubs are scattered about the room.

On the call of—Cumulus—All squat as for Grand Howl. (Cauliflower shape.)
—Cirrus—All stand on toes, arms held high. (Thin, wispy cloud.)
—Nimbo Stratus—All run to one end of room.
—Cumulo-Nimbus—All run to the other end of room.
—Stratus—All lie flat on the floor. (A layer of cloud.)

The Cub who is last will either be out or lose a point for his Six.

(*d*) **Clouds.**

Equipment needed: four chairs or logs

The Cubs are numbered in relay formation in the centre of the room. One chair or log is placed in each of the four corners of the room. Each chair represents a different type of cloud. Akela calls out a description of a cloud and a number, and the first boy to run round the correct chair and back to his Six wins a point.

(*e*) **Weather Vane.**

Equipment needed: none

Sixes are in line in their Six corners. Akela stands in the centre of the room facing north. On the call of 'the wind blows from the south', Sixes form up in a straight line facing north, Sixer with arms held out and hands together, Seconder with two arms flung back. The rest of the Six hold on to the boy's waist in front.

(*f*) **Compass Game.**

Equipment needed: sets of cards giving eight points of the compass

Divide the Pack into groups of eight. If there are a few boys over, make out duplicates of some of the points. Place cards face down in the centre of each group. On word 'Go' each boy takes a card. The boy with 'north' holds up his hand, and the rest place themselves in the correct position.

(*g*) **Trade Winds.**

Equipment needed: one square of paper per Cub
chalk

Each Cub makes a paper boat. The Pack is then divided into two halves. The first half line up their boats and on the

word 'Go' blow their boat into harbour (a chalk-line some distance away). The second half of the Pack have their turn. Have a final race between the winners.

ACTIVITIES.

Collect as many postcards, photographs or pictures from old calendars or greetings-cards that have a variety of different types of cloud. Ask the Cubs to look out for some as well.

Pack Activity.

(1) *Wall Frieze.* Cubs paste pictures on to lining-paper, writing the name of the cloud type under each. Make a frieze for your wall or let each Six decorate their own wall. Some of the smaller pictures and postcards can be stuck onto thick card and covered with sticky-backed plastic to be used as a training aid.

(2) For wall decoration or for flip-chart.

Large sheets of blue paper obtainable from any stationery shop, and cut in half make a good chart size.

Clouds are either flat, fibrous or fluffy, so a variety of materials can be used, i.e. cotton-wool, lint, tissue-paper, *Polyfilla*, a little black paint, etc.

Each piece of paper should have just one type of cloud on it, but the older Cubs might like to try charting the clouds with the help of the Scoutaids 'Clouds Recognition Chart'.

CUB SCOUT DISCOVERY CARD

Air resists objects moving in it.

You will need polythene
an old, large handkerchief or kitchen roll-tissue
string
a block of wood
a cup hook

(*a*) Throw the block of wood into the air and then note the speed at which it falls.

(*b*) Make a parachute and attach it to the block of wood. Throw it into the air and note the new speed at which it falls.

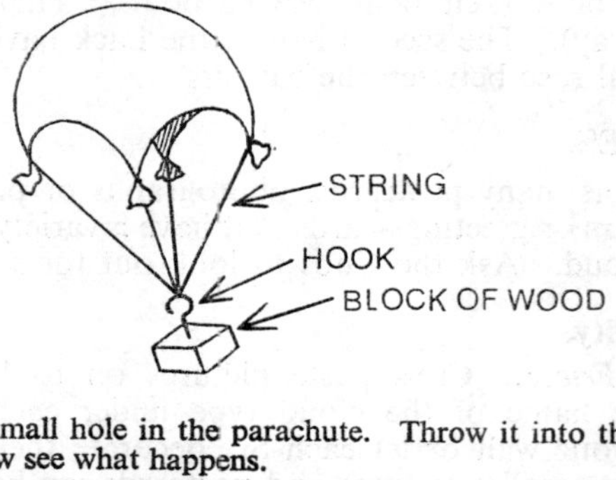

(*c*) Cut a small hole in the parachute. Throw it into the air again and now see what happens.

(*d*) Now gradually cut the hole larger and larger. What happens to the falling block as the hole gets bigger?

(3) Older Cub activity.

Any boy thinking of trying for the Photographer badge might like to try his hand at cloud pictures.

(4) With the help of the Ladybird Junior Science Book, *Air, Wind and Flight*, give each Six a different discovery card, and all the necessary equipment. (An explanation of this card is given opposite.) Perhaps one week the subject would be AIR; e.g. Red Six—which is the heaviest? Hot or cold air?; White Six—air resists objects moving in it; Blue Six—streamlining helps to overcome resistance, and so on for each Six. When all have had sufficient time, let each Six tell the rest of the Pack what they have found out.

A Discovery Card is just a postcard with the subject written clearly at the top, a list of equipment needed underneath, followed by questions or suggestions. (All equipment should be on a nearby table for collection by each Six.)

With regard to 'streamlining helps to overcome resistance', maybe the whole Pack could sketch their own ideas on either land, sea or aircraft.

Streamlining helps to overcome resistance.

Equipment needed: matches
candle
square block of wood
cocoa tin

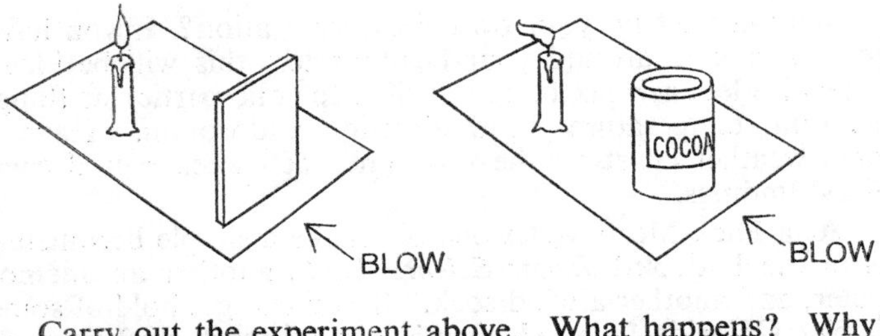

Carry out the experiment above. What happens? Why?

(5) Another week try AIR PRESSURE. Once again the same Ladybird Junior Science Book will help you, e.g. egg in a

bottle, the balloon and beaker, the tumbler of water, etc. Make out a Discovery Card for each Six. Another experiment the Cubs will enjoy doing is to fill a bucket with water, screw up a handkerchief and put it into a dry tumbler, and then plunge the tumbler, mouth down, into the bucket and back up again. The handkerchief remains dry. Why?

EVAPORATION.

Let the Cubs carry out an experiment at home. Tell them to put equal amounts of water in a jam-jar and in a wide dish. Ask them which evaporates faster.

WEATHER CHARTS.

Give each Cub a postcard divided up for seven days. Discuss together what symbols to use for different types of weather. Special symbols used to denote particular types of weather on a weather map can be found in *The Observer's Book of Weather*, by Reginald M. Lester (Frederick Warne & Co. Ltd.).

Snow ★ Hail △ Rain ● Blue sky ○ Cloudy sky ⦶ Fog ≡ and so on. Then ask each boy to draw these symbols along the top of the postcard. Underneath this write the days of the week. Let each boy take his chart home to fill in during the week.

WEATHER STATION.

Why not set up your own Weather Station? If you have your own land around your headquarters this will be ideal, otherwise let each Six be responsible for one particular thing, i.e. rain, temperature, wind direction and so on. Have a large weather chart on the wall, and each week record each Sixes' findings.

At a Pack Meeting, let one Six make a simple barometer, as in the Ladybird *Junior Science Book*, another an anemometer, and another a wind sock. If you can get hold of some Cobalt Chloride (a good chemist should stock this) let each boy draw and cut out a donkey on thick card, using string for his tail. Akela can then dip each tail into the liquid. The tail will be pink in fine weather and turn blue in wet weather.

LIGHTHOUSES.

If you want an excuse for a handcraft evening, bring in weather at sea and how it affects shipping. Use the Ladybird book of *Lighthouses, Lightships and Lifeboats* and read part of it to the Pack. Divide the Pack into age groups.

The ten-year-olds could each make a working lighthouse, and at the same time learn how to connect up a bulb to a battery.

Use a *Sifta Salt* or *Ajax* container on a square of hardboard. When the bulb in its holder has been connected to the two pieces of bell wire, and these have been passed down the container and out through the bottom, mix up plenty of *Polyfilla* to a stiff paste and cover the container, roughing it up to look like stone. Use small stones for rocks, fixing them with *Polyfilla*, and spreading the mixture over the hardboard to look like waves.

When dry it can be painted.

The nine-year-olds might like to make a foil picture of a lighthouse.

Foil Picture.

Equipment needed: cardboard
foil
string
Copydex

Each Cub draws a lighthouse on cardboard, with waves, birds, etc., keeping the outlines simple. He then glues along the outline, sticking down thin string as he goes. A square of foil three centimetres larger than the cardboard is placed, dull side up, on to the picture, the ends loosely folded under. A finger is then run down each side of the string outline, being very careful not to press too hard or the foil will tear.

This makes a very attractive picture.

Mosaic Lighthouse for Eight-year-olds.

Equipment needed: (1) egg-shells well washed
glue
paper
(2) tissue-paper
glue
paper

(1) Cubs draw a lighthouse and then crush egg-shells. The lighthouse is then glued all over and shells stuck into position. It can be painted when dry.

(2) Cubs draw a lighthouse and then glue it all over. Small pieces of tissue-paper are then screwed up, bit by bit, and placed in position on the lighthouse.

Collage Lighthouse.

Make a picture of a lighthouse, rocks, sea, clouds and birds, using odd scraps of material, wool, etc.

EXPLORER BADGE.

11-30 a.m. Cubs arrive.

Inspection of each boy's first-aid kit and footwear. Each Six under Scouter or Instructor collect wood and make a fire.

Cook Dinner.

Sixer has previously held a conference with his Six to decide on the menu, and who brings what food.

After the meal, Cubs make sure fires are out and the ground is tidied up.

Trail.

A sawdust trail is laid by a Sixer who hides within ten yards of the end of the trail until found.

Game : Back to Base.

Akela goes on ahead of the Pack who spread out and stalk him trying hard not to be seen, and at the same time mentally making a note of what Akela is doing (perhaps collecting different leaves, or picking up acorns, etc.). Akela occasionally stops, looks round and makes a note of which boys are spotted.

Back at Base.

Each Six chooses a site and builds a shelter. Everyone inspects shelters.

Tea.

In shelters.

Everyone clears and tidies ground.

Perhaps a suitable trophy or small prize to the Six which has gained the most points throughout the day.

This type of Meeting is, of course, easier for the country Pack than one in town, so how about getting together for a day and starting up an exchange of visits. A country Pack would like a day in town, too.

MAP READER BADGE.

Encourage the boys who have the Map Reader badge or are working on it, to plan a short ramble. Then let them take Akela and the rest of the Pack out one Saturday afternoon.

ST. GEORGE'S DAY. 23rd April.

Ideas for a Special Pack Meeting:

'St. George was a soldier and well-known for his bravery'—

Tournaments.

Equipment needed: white handkerchief

Two teams facing each other in pairs, one boy, a knight, mounted on the bigger boy, the horse. When the handkerchief is brought down by Akela, the two sides gallop towards each other. Two points if a knight removes the cap of one of the opposing knights, and five points if a knight is able to dismount one of the opposing side.

Display of Prowess.

Equipment needed: none

Two teams numbered and sitting facing each other.

When a number is called, those boys come forward, salute each other, and try to take hold of each other's ankles.

Six Activity.

Tableau—St. George.

Equipment needed: brown paper
old curtains
crêpe paper
cardboard
paper-clips
string, etc.

Each Six is given ten minutes to dress up and form a suitable tableau.

Game.

'St. George had to be very quiet on occasions in order to get nearer his enemy.'

Equipment needed: a sheet of paper.

Two teams at either end of the room. One Cub is chosen to be the enemy and sits in the centre of the room blindfolded. In front of him is a secret document. Akela nods to a boy from each team. They try to creep forward and tear a small piece of paper from the document and return to their teams without being heard and pointed at by the enemy. The team with the most pieces of document wins.

SPECIAL PACK MEETING.

Tramp evening and friends' night.

Grand gathering of Tramps.

Park Bench.

Equipment needed: none

'Tramps have to keep on the move when Police are about.'

Two teams facing each other and squatting on the ground. On the word 'Go' the first tramp from each team runs up and round the back of the other 'bench' (team) and then round

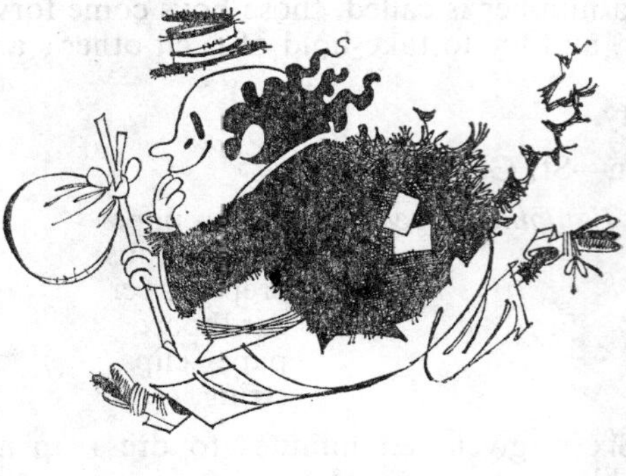

the back of his own bench and back to his place, when the second tramp runs up and round and so on to the end.

Secret Signs.

Equipment needed: none

'Tramps always leave signs on garden gates to warn future tramps of the type of hospitality to expect.'

Akela makes a series of signs with his arms, e.g.

Callers welcome		Cubs run to top of hall.
No food here	–	Cubs run to bottom of hall.
Fierce dog	–	Cubs curl up on the floor.
Police –	–	Cubs scatter to sides of hall.

Discovery.

Equipment required: one sheet of newspaper per boy

The newspaper is used like a blanket. Each tramp is given a sheet of newspaper. He then lies down and covers himself up with it. When the police whistle sounds, tramps must tear paper in half, fold each piece as small as possible and hide it on their person. Police (Scouters) try to find the paper.

Quick Hide. (A game to be played out of doors.)

Equipment needed: none

Tramps scatter on given signal. When the police whistle blows, all must hide immediately within a few yards. Police search for hidden tramps, and when found they aid the police in the capture of the others.

Police Bait.

'Tramps are always hungry.'

One sweet is placed in a bowl behind a Scouter. Tramps try and creep up to steal it. When Scouter looks round all freeze.

Old Shoes. Relay game.

Equipment needed: newspaper
string

Each tramp makes shoes from newspaper and string. Then a relay race is held.

Fires.

'Tramps like lighting fires. Sometimes barns catch fire.'

(Mention the danger of playing with fire.) Read a suitable yarn.

Eats.

Each boy will have a supply of food tied up in a large spotted handkerchief.

Sing-song.

'You can't put your muck in our dustbin' and 'Turnip Tops' are among many suitable songs.

Gardeners.

How about getting the whole Pack interested in gardening by holding 'A Best Kept Patch of Garden' competition, one class for vegetables, and one for flowers.

You will find the parents entering into this with great enthusiasm. It may be, however, that you have one or two boys without a garden, but here Akela or an Assistant might care to give up a corner of their own garden.

Don't let the boys' interest flag; pay regular visits to their gardens, and run the occasional garden quiz. Have discussions on tools, and have games bringing in flowers, weeds, pests, etc.

Shrove Tuesday—Pancakes.

Why not hold a competition for the most original filling to be brought along to the Pack meeting. Each Sixer could bring enough batter mixture for his Six, but it is advisable for Scouters to bring extra, as Cub appetites are large!

KNOW YOUR DISTRICT. Town.

Spread this activity over several weeks, using an occasional Saturday where necessary.

Each Six should have a 'master map' of the town stuck down on to a piece of hardboard leaving an inch margin all round. A thin piece of paper can then be placed over the map for the Cubs to mark in pillar-boxes, telephone kiosks, etc. Cubs should also have quarto-sized hardboard with paper clipped to it for any sketching or notes. The result of this is much neater work.

Divide the activities into past and present. There should

be a good deal of careful planning by the Scouters well beforehand. Visit your local library for information on your neighbourhood, contact the local historical society if one exists near you, visit supermarkets, garages, churches and whatever places you hope to include in this project. The Cubs should work in their Sixes, with each Six on a different project. The following are some ideas which, of course, will need to be altered to suit your area:

Cars.

(1) Mark on your map all the public car-parks. How many cars does each hold? Are all the car-parks free ones?

(2) How many garages serve the motorist in this town, and what brand and grade of petrol do they sell?

(3) Is there a car-hire firm in the town?

Inns and Public Houses.

(1) Mark on your map all public houses. Make a list of the names and sketch the signs.

(2) Which is the oldest building? Does it have any history?

Views of Your Town.

Equipment needed: camera, film

Photograph interesting buildings and scenes in your town. Make a note of each exposure.

Sounds in Your Town.

Equipment needed: tape recorder, cassette.

Walk around your town and listen and record typical sounds in your town.

Schools:

(1) How many schools in your town? Mark them in on your map.

(2) Name each school and give the age group and number of pupils.

Places of Worship.

(1) How many places of worship are there in your town? Mark them in on your map.

(2) Visit one and find out about its history.

Arrange visits to Police station, library, factory, church, etc., for each Six, and then let them entertain the rest of the Pack with their findings.

Parents' Evening.

You now have all you need for a most entertaining Parents' Evening based on knowledge of your district and local history, i.e. show colour-slides with a running commentary by the Cubs, and bringing in tape recordings of sounds, interviews, dialects, etc.

Play-acting, in costume, an episode in history connected with your town. Your headquarters should be decorated with maps, photographs and all the information that has been learned.

Summer

IDEAS FOR SUMMER MONTHS.

Whatever idea or subject you hit upon for your summer expeditions, you may be lucky enough to find just the right person with the expert knowledge you need. If no such person is forthcoming, then become an expert yourself. Go to your local library and get out all the books you can on the subject. The children's section is worth exploring.

Ideas for Pack Meetings and special activities can be found anywhere. The local newspaper will give you places of interest, special shows or displays suitable for children, and will most likely list societies and clubs. Perhaps a local historical society exists in your neighbourhood. The local radio run special programmes on where to take children, and give information on local exhibitions, theatres, outings, etc.

Heritage Publications in association with New English Library have brought out three paperbacks written by R. L. & M. J. Elliott entitled:-

Where To Go What To Do in the S.E.—covering Kent, Sussex and Surrey, plus London, South of the Thames.

Where To Go What To Do in the South—covering Dorset, Hants, Isle of Wight, Wiltshire and part of Somerset.

Where To Go What To Do in the S.W.—covering Devon, Cornwall and part of Somerset.

These are excellent little books for a Scouter to add to his Pack Library. The South Edition gives the basic facts of nearly 500 places to visit, 200 of these providing shelter from our inclement weather.

BOATS.

Ask the Cubs to make any type of river-craft they like, not larger than 12 inches long. This can be done any time during the week with father joining in the fun.

At the next Pack Meeting, make your way to the nearest pond or stream and hold a race. (Wellington boots are advisable!)

There will, no doubt, be quite an assortment of craft—yachts, rafts, steamers, and warships, etc. Perhaps a small prize can be given to the most 'seaworthy craft'.

CUB AND PARENT PICNIC.

This can be a wonderful afternoon, but a good deal of careful planning and preparation is necessary. Food can either be brought by individual families, or the older Cubs can do some cooking over open fires. Many ideas for games and activities will come to mind, with Dads and Mums joining in.

KITE FLYING (Discovering).

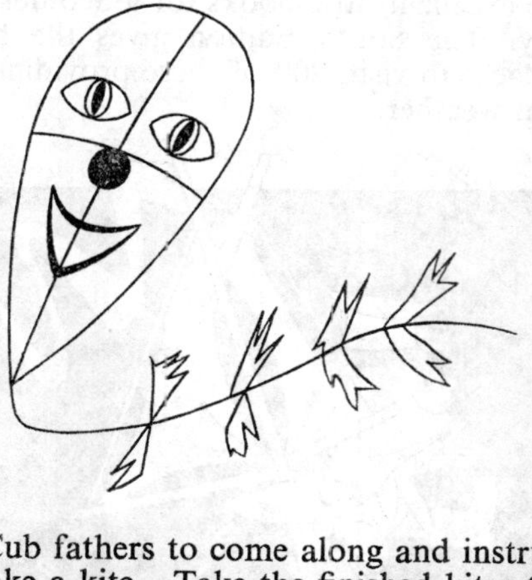

Ask two Cub fathers to come along and instruct the boys on how to make a kite. Take the finished kites to the beach or high ground to fly them. Most farmers have endless empty meal bags which they do not want. If you can get hold of some, they make excellent paper for kites, and have many other uses in a pack when opened out, e.g. scrapbooks, drawing paper, flip charts, etc.

LEAVES (Collector Badge).

Make a leaf collection in any of the following ways-

(*a*) Mount the leaf on card, cover with *Fablon*, and seal round the edges with *Sellotape*.

(*b*) **Carbon leaf prints.** Place a sheet of white paper on the table, and then a sheet of carbon paper over it. Put the leaf carefully on to the carbon paper and cover it with newspaper. Then, with a warm iron gently rub over the newspaper.

(*c*) **Plaster Prints.**

Equipment needed: postcards
Polyfilla mixture
Vaseline
leaves

Cover the card with the *Polyfilla* mixture, using an old knife. (The mixture should be thick paste and not runny.) Vaseline the leaf and press it carefully into the mixture. Leave the *Polyfilla* to harden and then remove the leaf, leaving a perfect print.

(*d*) **Waxing Leaves.**

Equipment needed: saucepan
candle-wax
cooker

Heat the wax in a saucepan over a gentle heat until it has melted. Dip the leaves in one at a time, holding the stem, then tie a piece of string to the leaf and hang it up to dry.

(*e*) **Leaf Rubbings.**

Place a sheet of paper over a leaf and rub gently with the side of a lead pencil.

NATURE COMPETITION.

Try running a nature competition over a period of say two months, with an Observer book as prize. At the end of each Meeting, tell the Cubs what you want for the following week, e.g. a collection of named leaves, a collection of grasses, named if possible, three fishes drawn and described, etc. In rural Packs, Akela might be able to find a snake skin to take along to show the boys, and perhaps skulls of small animals and skeletons of birds. The Scouters should in any case join in these weekly competitions, and they will no doubt learn a good deal. Have a nature table in the corner of your headquarters where all the weekly collections can be put on show. Have several reference books on hand to help with the naming of exhibits.

SPECIAL EVENING.

One Pack Meeting lay a trail for each Six leading to a particular spot. Then let your boys have the great pleasure of cooking sausages on sticks over open fires, or perhaps a bean and sausage sizzle, with each Six using one large frying-pan. If you finish the evening with hot cocoa, a short yarn and a camp fire, this will make an evening long remembered by your Cubs.

DISCOVERY.

Let each Six go off on a journey of discovery and give them the necessary equipment.

WHITE SIX—*Insects and small animals.*

'Look under large stones and among grasses.'

Equipment needed: small jars
trowel
notebooks
pencils
reference book

RED SIX—*Birds.*

'How many types of birds are there in a given area? Record any bird song; collect any feathers lying around; do some sketches.'

Equipment needed: notebooks
pencils
cassette recorder
reference book

BLUE SIX—*Grasses.*

'How many different grasses can you find?'

Equipment needed: exercise book in which to place grasses
pencil
reference book

TREASURE HUNT (Observation).

Make a collection of cotton reels, and draw a coloured band round each one with a felt-tip pen to represent each Six. During an outdoor Meeting hold a treasure hunt by tucking a

piece of paper with one word on it into each cotton reel. Hide these reels on branches of trees and in bushes within a certain area. When the words are removed and placed in a certain order they give the hiding-place of the treasure, perhaps a bag of apples.

ANIMAL ZOO (Observation and Imagination).

SIX ACTIVITY.

When out on a Cub expedition, look out for the oddly shaped sticks that might perhaps resemble animals. Break off any branches or twigs which are not needed, and perhaps add eyes and a little colour to your animals.

MINIATURE GARDEN.

This can be a Six activity during an out of doors evening Meeting. Either supply each Six with a seed box or let them mark out an area on the ground. With twigs, leaves, stones, moss, etc., it is possible to make a very attractive garden.

NATURE COLLECTION (Discovering).

Give each boy an egg box. Ask him to go off and find something for each compartment that he has never seen before or heard anything about. Take along reference books, but if something cannot be named, make it a challenge for the following week, with each boy trying to find out the name and a bit about it.

TRAILS.

These are always popular with boys, and remembering to keep the countryside tidy, use perhaps sawdust or one certain leaf. Maybe the stem could point in the direction to be followed. Wool trails are a good idea if the wool used is of each Six colour. The Six would then follow the trail and collect up the wool as they went along. Points for largest collection of wool.

COUNTRY CODE.

Hold a poster competition on the Country Code. Give each Six something different, e.g. guard against fire, fasten all gates, keep to the paths, do not leave your litter behind, etc.

COLLECTING GRASSES.

A Six competition for the most varied collection. Most common are Timothy, Rye Grass, Cock's Foot, Bentz (or water grass).

MOWGLI NECKLACE.

Make a necklace of perhaps acorns, or conkers, shells, buttons, seeds from the garden, or even safety-pins. Present this to the smartest Cub after each weekly inspection.

OLYMPIC GAMES.

A great many Districts hold a Cub Sports Day, and for a week or two before the event Packs are busy making trial runs and picking their teams for this big day. This can tend to become a bit chaotic—measuring ground, getting boys into age groups, etc., so why not disguise the whole thing and hold an Olympic Games? Each Six can represent a country, e.g. Australia, France, Germany, etc., and might even try to make their own flag, using lining paper. To begin your evening have a grand parade of all the countries. When an event is announced, each 'country' sends in one or two boys of the right age group. Put in several team games to keep the whole thing going without a stop. A Cub Instructor can keep the score and at the end of the evening will read out the winning country and the winners of the individual events. Perhaps

D

you could invite a member of the Group Executive Committee along to present the medals—Kilner jar tops painted gold, silver or bronze with yellow or white wool threaded through a punched hole.

A DIG (Gardener Badge).

Organise a Pack Dig—for worms, and perhaps make your own Wormery using a large glass jar, or better still, an old aquarium. Fill up whichever container you choose with alternate layers of soil, sand and leafmould. On top of this put some vegetable matter. Do not overcrowd your wormery. Keep it damp, but not wet.

THREEPENNY PARTY.

To run a Pack well, funds must be readily available. A realistic weekly subscription is a good start, and if your Pack hasn't run a ten pence party you should certainly try one. It is enormous fun and quite profitable. Send out invitations to parents and friends. Charge ten pence entrance, and then have as many sideshows as you can think of, charging ten pence a go. For example:

(*a*) How many times a candle can be lighted with only one match.

(*b*) Fixing a tail on a donkey while blindfolded.

(*c*) Hearing your voice on a cassette recorder.
(*d*) How many stitches can be cast on a needle in a given time.
(*e*) Skittles.

There are many, many more you can think up.

Refreshments could be on sale at various prices and there could perhaps be a jumble stall.

SEASHORE ACTIVITIES.

Many a Scouter, on arriving on the seashore with a Pack of excited boys, will just find a good spot to settle down for a well deserved rest, and spend the rest of the day in lazy observation of his boys whilst they swim, paddle or just rush around. However, there are many exciting activities that all can join in.

Biggest Sand-castle Competition.

Make this a Six event, with ice-cream or a stick of rock for the winning Six.

Collecting Seaweeds.

There are over 700 seaweeds to be found round the British Isles and a book from your local library should help you to identify them.

Seaweeds are divided into three main groups—red, brown and green. The red seaweeds are often found in deep water and the green seaweed is high up on the beach. The brown seaweed is found somewhere between the two. If they are carefully rinsed in the sea and then placed in a plastic bag and put in a shady place until it is time to go home, they should arrive back in good condition. The salt water should then be rinsed from the seaweeds before they are carefully mounted on card for display. The mounting is best done in water, as the seaweeds then fall into natural positions.

Collection of Stones.

There are many beautiful stones to be found on our beaches, and it is well worth your while to take a book along

with you to help identify the different kinds. They are easier to identify when wet. To keep that wet look, let the Cubs varnish each stone at one Pack Meeting.

Ducks and Drakes.

This is a popular game with children and adults alike. Choose a flat stone and, with a flick of the wrist, send your stone flat across the water and see how many times you can make it jump on the surface. This game is not meant for a crowded beach.

Exploration of Pools.

In almost any pool left by the receding tide, there are a host of exciting things to be found, e.g. anemones, crabs, many fish, etc. Let each Six, with a Scouter in charge, see what they can find.

Sandy Beach.

Digging on a sandy beach can produce a wealth of tiny animal life.

Dams and Waterways.

A great deal of fun can be had when there is an incoming tide.

I Spy.

Give each Six an *I Spy on the Seashore* book and see how much they can discover.

Cricket and Football.

These should, of course, only be played when you have a stretch of beach to yourselves.

Collection of Sea-shells.

Collect as many shells as you can, and later make a wall-chart for your headquarters, naming as many shells as possible. If these are varnished they will give the appearance of being wet.

Shells can also be used in many ways during a winter Pack Meeting, e.g. making Christmas presents by covering boxes or plant pots with *Polyfilla* and placing the shells into position. They can either be painted or varnished when dry. Or perhaps making shell pictures on card, using sand and various seeds or pebbles as well.

Here is a list of books which you might find useful for your seashore activities:

Sea Shells of the World, by R. Tucker Abbott, Ph.D. and Herbert S. Zim, Ph.D. (Paul Hamlyn. 160 pp.)

The Seashore and Seashore Life. A Ladybird Book. (Wills & Hepworth Ltd.)

A Guide to the Seashore, by Ray Ingle. (Paul Hamlyn. 160 pp.)

Discovering Sea Shells, by Barry Charles. (Shire Publications. 56 pp.)

The Pebbles on the Beach, by Clarence Ellis. (Faber & Faber Ltd. 164 pp. Paperback).

POND DIPPING.

Equipment needed
- wellington boots
- fishing-net (home-made are stronger)
- two jam-jars with string handles
- Ladybird book on Pond Life
- first-aid kit
- insect repellent

Try and have at least two visits to the same pond or stream during the spring and summer months, so that the Cubs can note the difference. It is sometimes found easier to use a jam-jar rather than a net for catching your shrimps or water-beatles. There is always something to be found under a stone in a stream. Every Cub should find something.

SPIDER HUNT.

First of all make your spider cage.

Equipment needed: one shallow cake-tin with lid
fine wire mesh
Polyfilla

Measure the wire to fit round the inside of the tin. Next mix the *Polyfilla* to a thick paste and put it into the bottom of the tin. Stand the wire back into position and join the edges together with a thin piece of wire. You can add a few twigs into the mixture at this stage for the spiders to attach their webs to. When the *Polyfilla* is set, put the lid of the tin on top. When you have caught your spiders, remember that they need a daily water supply, but can go without food for weeks. Food consists of small, live insects.

KNOW YOUR DISTRICT.

This Arrow activity can become a very exciting Pack project that can go on for as long as you wish and, at the same time, bring in the following badges and Arrow activities:

Local History	Discovering Nature
Artist Badge	Map Reader Badge
Photographer Badge	Book Reader Badge
Simple Collection	Telephone Message
Animal Lover Badge	

First of all, make a very large scrapbook. This will become your very own town or village guide-book.

Ideas for the book are endless:

(*a*) A sketch map of, say, one kilometre radius of your headquarters.

(Map Reader Badge)

(*b*) Make a collection of pressed leaves, flowers and grasses in your area.

(Discovering)

(*c*) Drawings of church, school, your headquarters, Town Hall, etc.

(Discovering & Artist Badge)

(*d*) Photographs of local views and important persons. Buy a film out of Pack funds.

(Photographer Badge)

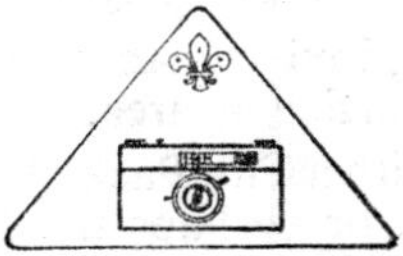

(*e*) Visit a library or invite along an old local inhabitant or a member of the local Historical Society to talk on local history.

(Exploring and Book Reader Badge)

(*f*) Telephone local youth leaders, club members, etc., to find out about meeting places and times.

(*g*) Interview publican, postman, policeman, fireman, etc. A cassette recorder would be an asset.

(*h*) Careful observation of various birds in your area, by setting up bird tables.

(Discovering & Animal Lover Badge)

(*i*) Make a map of local ponds and streams.

(Map Reader Badge)

(*j*) Perhaps the Rector would show a Six over the church and relate some of its history. The Cubs might be given permission to do some brass rubbings.

(Artist Badge)

Maybe this has inspired you to go on and plan out your own ideas to fit your particular area.

If you have a link with a Cub Pack abroad, this book would make a wonderful gift, or perhaps the Rector would like the book displayed on a table at the back of the church for the benefit of visitors during the summer months.

ANIMAL LOVER BADGE—Birds.

Six activities: (simple collection).

(*a*) **Feathers.**

Ask the Cubs to collect as many different kinds of feathers as they can during the week. Feathers can teach Cubs a lot about birds and how to identify them. Try and persuade a local ornithologist to come along to your Pack Meeting to help you to recognise from which birds the feathers come, and also what part of the bird. These can either be mounted directly into a boy's scrapbook, or mounted on a postcard or bigger card and covered with *Fablon*. This latter way means that they can be used for games or display.

(*b*) **Bird Identification.**

Equipment needed: card cut-outs of birds in flight clearly named
black paper
sheets of blue paper
glue
scissors
pencils

Each boy draws round the card outline of a bird on to black paper. Then he carefully cuts this out, and sticks it on to a sheet of blue paper. Several birds can go on one sheet. Label the birds if you wish. These charts can be used for games or display.

(*c*) **Bird Migration.**

Equipment needed: large sheet of paper with outline drawing of different countries, or maps of the world

Use coloured felt tip pens to mark the direction birds travel and the time of the year. Small cut out pictures of the birds would make the chart more colourful and easier to learn from.

(*d*) **Beaks, Bills and Feet.**

Using the Ladybird book, *Birds and how they live*, each Six makes its own wall-chart.

(*e*) **Bird Song.**

(1) Records—Try and find a large photograph of the birds to show on your flip-chart as each song is heard.
(2) Make your own recordings.

(*f*) **Taxidermist.**

Perhaps one of your Cub parents or friends is a taxidermist and would bring his collection of birds to a Pack Meeting.

(*g*) **Bird Tables or Nesting Boxes.**

(Handyman Badge)

Let the boys decide what they want to do and ask for a few volunteer fathers. Discuss what wood and tools are needed and the following week spend your Pack Meeting making these.

(*h*) **Bird Food.**

Equipment needed: cooking stoves
large mixing bowls
wooden spoons
large saucepans

The Cubs are asked to bring any scraps from home—bacon rind, bits of meat, crumbs, biscuits, fat, dripping, porridge oats, etc., plus one medium-sized flower-pot.

Put all the mixtures into saucepans and, although this looks quite revolting, the delicious smell that escapes from your headquarters will make neighbours think you are cooking some wonderful meal. Attach some string to each flower-pot through the bottom hole. Take the mixture off the stove and, when it begins to set, pack it into each flower-pot and leave to harden. Tell the Cubs to hang their pots upside down, well out of reach of cats.

(*i*) **Bird Study.**

Let the Pack choose a bird, and then collect all the information they can on its behaviour, where it builds its nest, what food it eats, the number seen, etc.

The Young Ornithologists' Club.

If sufficient of your Cubs are interested in birds, why not ask them if they would like to join the Young Ornithologists Club. Group membership is 50p each (a minimum of ten) and includes a cloth arm badge. Outings and Y.O.C. holiday courses are run for members, and a quarterly magazine (one, for every ten members) called *Bird Life*, contains a number of projects, competitions and interesting articles. For further details write to—The Education Office, R.S.P.B., The Lodge, Sandy, Beds.

The R.S.P.B. have brought out a very useful small book called *Bird Projects for Schools*. There is plenty here to keep you busy. Another book that is an absolute mine of information is *The Bird Table Book*, by Tony Soper (Pan Books Ltd.).

HOLIDAY ACTIVITY—August.

Ask the Cubs to make a day by day collection connected with their holiday activities.

Give them plenty of ideas—A bus ticket from a day's outing, a timetable, sketches of buildings or wild-life, shells after a visit to the coast, feathers, postcards, etc. Encourage the boys to date each item and, if possible, to stick them in order in a scrapbook.

On the first Meeting after the holiday, have a table ready to display all the collections and let the boys talk about their finds.

BARK RUBBINGS—Six Activity.

Send each Six out with a supply of paper and thick wax crayons. A bark rubbing will be a lot neater if one boy holds the paper against the trunk and the other boy covers the paper with firm strokes in one direction. The name of the

tree and the date of the rubbing should be written on the top of the page. Each Six could then mount these papers on a large sheet of dark paper for display purposes, or maybe these rubbings could be put into the sixes scrapbook as their nature logbook.

SEEDS—Pack Activity.

Ask the Cubs to collect seeds from their gardens, being careful to keep each type separate. When dried these can be put into small envelopes and clearly labelled, ready for planting again next spring.

You could very well follow on from here with a discussion on seed dispersal; seeds which travel by air, e.g. ash, elm, which have wings, dandelion seeds which float along, seeds with tiny hooks which cling to animals and man before dropping to the ground or into rivers and streams. Birds also carry seeds, and even squirrels help. Make a list and do some sketches as well as making a collection of the different types of seeds.

PIRATE EVENING.

Pull down the Union Flag and hoist the Jolly Roger (made by some of the Cubs the previous week).

All give three cheers.

Parade of the Pirates—Small prize for the fiercest-looking pirate.

Port and Starboard.

Equipment needed: none

The four walls of your headquarters are—port, starboard, fore and aft. Captain's coming—salute, big wave coming over—flat on backs, bombs overhead—crouch on floor, hands over head, feet off deck—either jump on to a chair or lie on backs with feet up, man the lifeboats—run into groups of whatever number is called.

Ships Ahoy!

Equipment needed: tent pegs
lining paper
Scout staves
felt tip pens
rope

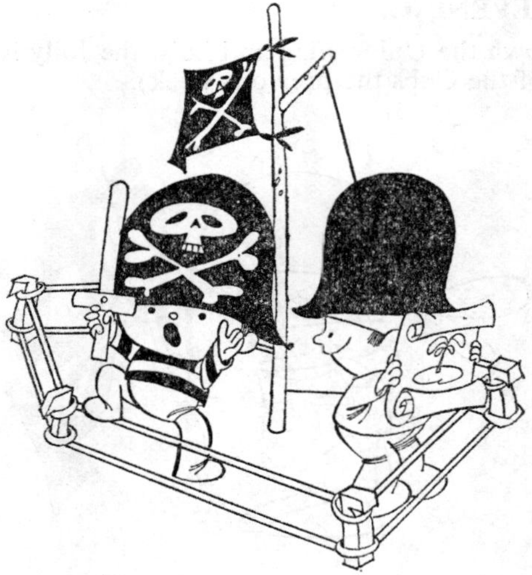

Each Six makes its own ship and names it, e.g. Grey Six—Grey Phantom; Black Six—Black Jack; White Six—White Hawk; Red Six—Red Devil, and so on.

Ball of Fire.

Equipment needed: large ball

Large circle of pirates, savages in the centre. Pirates try to hit the savages below the knee with 'ball of fire'.

Walking the Plank.

This is a relay game with the plank being whatever you

happen to have to hand. Perhaps a row of chairs close together, a bench or even a thick rope.

Treasure Hunt.

With a bag of chocolate money hidden at the end of the trail.

Yarn.

A story about adventure at sea.

Sing-song.

Pirates are Pardoned.

Pack changes back into Cub uniform, pulls down the Jolly Roger and hoists the Union Flag.

Prayers.

Autumn

BLACKBERRY JAM—September.

Ask the Cubs to pick as many blackberries as they can and to bring them, plus as many jam-jars as their mothers can spare, to the next Pack Meeting. Try and get hold of one cooker per Six.

Maybe parents can help on this, or perhaps the Scouts have calor gas cookers. It is advisable to have one Scouter or adult helper per Six, and all wearing aprons.

Equipment suggested: blackberries
sugar
jam-jars
large saucepans
wooden spoons
water
labels
washing-up liquid
towels
teacloths
thermometer (optional)
colanders
measuring jugs
scales

When the jam is set, get in touch with a local Children's Home, and ask if they will accept the jam. Children would be better than old people because of the seeds.

CLOTHES-PEGS.

With the old type of clothes-peg, hold a competition for the most original doll. This is something that can be done at home with parents joining in the fun.

If you have any trouble getting the pegs, write to Merchant Chandler, 72 New Kings Road, Parsons Green, London, S.W.6.

PARENTS' PARTICIPATION.

Most parents enjoy taking an active part in their son's Scout Group. This does not mean just becoming Council members, serving teas or helping to repair the Scout headquarter's roof, but being familiar with all the Arrow requirements and joining in the various Group activities. Here are a few suggestions:

(*a*) You will, as a matter of course, visit all parents of new Cubs, but put them fully in the picture with regard to Arrows and Badges and what part they can play.

(*b*) Invite the parents along to their son's Investiture, but make quite sure first of all that the boy wants this.

(*c*) During the summer months arrange a Cub and parent picnic.

(*d*) Have a Father and Son evening.

(*e*) Hold a Mother and Son evening near to Mothering Sunday and let the boys give their Mums small presents or cards they have made at a previous Pack Meeting.

(*f*) Use *Scoutaids Parents Help Slips.*

(*g*) Look for Badge Examiners among your parents.

(*h*) If you get to know the parents well, you will, no doubt, discover all sorts of hobbies and interests that will be of help in Pack activities.

(*i*) Send out a monthly Group News Letter. Perhaps a special Parent Magazine Committee would organise this. In the News Letter tell the parents what you are doing in your weekly Pack Meetings, names of boys who have gained various Arrow requirements, or badges, etc. Let the Cubs contribute something, perhaps drawings and details of a recent outing or special project. Why not hold a competition for the best cover for the News Letter and encourage all families to enter?

(*j*) Occasionally, instead of the usual weekly Pack Meeting in your headquarters, let each Six or age group meet in a parent's home. For example, maybe Mr. Smith of your

Group Executive Committee would have half-a-dozen boys in his workshop for handcraft and use and care of tools, whilst Mr. Tester, White Sixer's father, is doing photography in his dark-room with a small group, and Mrs. Freeman, a Cub Mum and ex-nurse, is instructing on first aid in her home. Another group or Six could be making puppets and a theatre, and another doing the Scientist Badge requirements in other homes.

(*k*) **Family Coach Trip.** Perhaps a Circus or Pantomime, or maybe an outing to the coast in the summer months.

(*l*) **Recipe Book.** Ask the Cubs to bring along any of their mother's favourite recipes. Either put these, a few at a time, into your monthly News Letter, or let the Sixers arrange these into a scrapbook with perhaps some appropriate pictures. Copies could be made of these and sold at your next Parents' Evening.

(*m*) **Swimming.** Cub fathers would perhaps take small groups of boys to the nearest swimming-baths and give swimming instruction.

CUB SCOUT CHALLENGE.

Whatever your Meeting you will always find that there is either no time to complete something, or else it is not possible to do a certain project with only one and a half hours at your disposal or without the necessary facilities. This is where the CUB SCOUT CHALLENGE is useful. All children love a challenge and will be eager to complete each week's new one.

Tell the parents all about these Challenges and that, although you do not, of course, want them to complete the challenge for their sons, you would like them to encourage and help look things up and supply the necessary equipment. Soon you will find most parents entering into the fun. Perhaps a small prize of a Ladybird book could be given at the end of so many challenges.

Fix a large sheet of paper on the wall with a list of boys' names down the left-hand side. Give five points for a completed challenge with perhaps an extra point or two for anything that has had a great deal of work put into it.

A few examples—Supposing your monthly theme is 'weather', perhaps your challenge could be:

(*a*) See how many postcards or photographs you can collect which include different cloud formations;

(*b*) Put some ice-cubes into a shiny tin and sprinkle some salt on them to make them even colder. Wait awhile, now what do you see on the outside of the tin? Where have these come from?

(*c*) Water evaporation. Put the same amount of water into a tall vase and a cereal bowl. Which evaporates the fastest? Why?

(*d*) Give each boy a postcard divided up into seven days. This is his own Weather Chart. Put the code along the top as explained on page 16.

THRIFT.

Give each boy 20p and tell them they have one week to make it grow. The Cubs will be most enthusiastic and perhaps you will find them buying wooden boxes from the grocer and splitting them up into bundles of firewood, making wooden toys for babies, or even attending jumble sales to resell items at a profit!

PRAYERS (Thinking).

Give each Cub a piece of white card, ask them to write out either their favourite prayer or one they have made up and bring it to the next Pack Meeting. Each boy then takes it in turn to read his own prayer, week by week. You might even find among them a prayer that you can keep as your own special Pack prayer. Why not let the Sixers stick the prayers into a scrapbook with an appropriate picture alongside?

PARENTS' EVENING.

1830 hours. Grand Howl, Flag Break.
Inspection. (Explain to the parents what you look for, the correct length of scarf, etc.).

Present the Mowgli Necklace to the smartest Cub. (This was explained on page 37 as being a necklace, made by the Cubs, and consisting of either shells, beads, seeds, etc.).

Action Man (A Warming-up Game).

Equipment needed: none

'Quick Fire'	—	stamp feet and whirl round and round.
'Shell Fire'	—	everyone crouches down.
'Tanks'	—	on all fours to top of hall.
'Jeeps'	—	run to bottom of hall.
'Surrender'	—	arms above head.
'Enemy'	—	scatter to sides of hall.

Leaf Relay (Nature).

Equipment needed: collection of leaves for each Six

Relay formation numbered. A collection of leaves is placed some yards in front of each Six. Scouter calls the name of a leaf and a number. Boys run forward, pick up the correct leaf and run to Scouter.

Demonstration of Arrow Scheme.

Cubs get into ready-prepared places, where equipment is all to hand. A running commentary is given by Akela on each Group's activity, e.g.:

GROWING UP—'Helps to develop the boy's own ability, and helps him to become self-reliant.'

Three Sports Training Activities—Demonstration of skipping, somersault, leapfrog, etc.

Simple First-Aid—A group of boys packing a first-aid kit for a Pack Outing. One Cub treating a graze and another putting on a large arm sling.

Observation Game—A small circle of Cubs playing a simple Kim's Game.

Lay a Trail—Boys getting to know the various tracking signs using sticks and stones.

Compass—Cubs sitting round a O.S. Map and using a compass.

Health—Knowing the right kind of foods to eat. Pictures of food being glued on to large sheets of paper, one sheet containing the wrong type of foods to eat too much of, and the other sheet containing the correct foods to encourage.

Toothbrush and the Germ—Health.

Circle of boys representing teeth. One boy is a toothbrush and is outside the circle, and one boy is the Germ and is inside the circle. The Toothbrush has to try and catch the Germ. The teeth try and stop the Toothbrush getting through, but if he succeeds, they let the Germ go to the outside, and so on. When the Germ is caught, two new boys are chosen.

Demonstration of Arrow Scheme.

DISCOVERING—'Helps the boy to gain self-confidence and to find out his capabilities. Also gives him some basic Scouting skills.'

Knotting—A group doing round turn and two half hitches and a bowline.

Union Flag—Cubs with a Cub Instructor learning about the three crosses on the Union Flag, and perhaps how to fold the flag.

Three Scientific Experiments—Cubs carrying out any of the experiments from the Ladybird Junior Science Books.

Bicycle Maintenance—Cubs learning how to tighten a chain.

Nature—With a Cub Instructor on hand, one Cub places a carrot top on to a saucer of gravel and adds some water, whilst another Cub scatters seed on to a dish containing damp lint. Another boy could be filling up an old orange net with fat for Tits.

24-hour Clock—Cubs learning the time from a large card-board clock. Another two Cubs could be looking through a rail timetable.

Shoe-Stuffing Relay—Help at Home.

Equipment needed: one pair of adult shoes per Six
newspaper

First boy of each Six runs up and stuffs the pair of shoes, then runs back and touches off number two, who runs up and takes the stuffing out. And so on down the Six.

Demonstration of Arrow Scheme.

THINKING—'Helps the Cub Scout to find out how he can help others, and what society expects of him.'

Miming—People whose job it is to help others—fireman, doctor, lifeboatman, etc. Cub Instructor sitting in with boys here.

Advertisements—Two large sheets of paper and a pile of advertisements cut from magazines. Cubs stick on to one sheet advertisements they feel have impact, and on the other, advertisements they feel would not sell that particular product.

Communication—A Cub sending a short message in semaphore. A small group of boys sitting a short distance away taking down the message.

Poster—Cubs putting the finishing touches to a poster advertising Cub Scouting.

Litter—Cubs constructing a model from toilet rolls, cartons, etc.

Another Country—Cubs sitting round a large flannelgraph map of a foreign country trying to fix in the correct position of the various towns.

Highway Code (Cyclist Badge).

Equipment needed: beans

Have a small collection of beans some distance from each Six. Scouter calls out road sign and number. That number runs forward and makes the sign with the beans.

Demonstration of Arrow Scheme.

SHARING—'Helps the Cub Scout to learn to give and take, and to co-operate with others, thereby learning to recognise his own, as well as others, abilities.'

Telephone—An old telephone being used to practise 999 calls. Two other boys might be testing each other on the use of a directory and code book.

Accidents in the Home—Cubs sitting in a circle. In the centre a number of objects that could prove dangerous. After looking at the objects for a few minutes, they are covered up. Boys list their finds, and say how they could be dangerous if in their home, i.e. pills with lid off, frayed flex, razor blade, roller-skate, box of matches, etc.

Weather—One Cub making a barometer and another constructing a weather-vane. Instructions are in Air, Wind and Flight, a Ladybird Junior Science Book.

Folding Scarf Correctly—Some of the younger Cubs with a Cub Instructor.

Traffic-signs and Symbols—A Sixer with a home-made flip chart of symbols, with one or two other Cubs saying what each symbol means.

Television Programmes—Cubs dressed up and acting something from their favourite programme.

Circle Airlines (Discovering).

Equipment needed: bean bag

Boys named round circle in fours—

Aer Lingus—Pan Am—Quantas—El Al.

Airline is called by Scouter. Those boys run round the circle clockwise, and in through their own gap to grab the bean bag.

Parade Circle—Presentation of any Arrows or Badges.
Grand Howl, Flag Down, Prayers.

HALLOWE'EN EVENING.

This is not quite so popular here as in America, but it is a wonderful excuse for a Special Pack Meeting.

Your imagination could really run riot with decorations—cut-outs of witches on broomsticks, bats, owls, etc., hanging from the ceiling, black and orange crêpe paper decorating the lights, and black wool or garden nets resembling cobwebs. The boys could, no doubt, think of more ideas for you, and will, of course, enjoy making them.

Let the Cubs come in a costume of their choice—devils, ghosts, wizards, cats, etc. It is, however, very important for them to change out of their costume at the end of the Special Pack Meeting, and to finish in the usual way with Grand Howl and Prayers. Maybe you could make this Hallowe'en Evening your Father and Son Meeting, in which case let the Cubs design their own invitation cards to give to their fathers.

The following is a suggested Pack Meeting:

HALLOWE'EN EVENING. October.

Special Pack Meeting.

(The previous week each Cub makes a suitable invitation card to give to his father.)

7 p.m. The witches, wizards, ghosts and devils arrive with their fathers.

Witches Nose.

Equipment needed: one large drawing per Six of a witch without her nose.
one cardboard-hooked nose per Six

Each boy runs up to drawing, shuts his eyes, is turned twice by the Scouter and then tries to pin the nose in the correct position. Cubs first and then their fathers.

Shadows.

Equipment needed: large sheet or curtain with light behind

Boys walk behind the curtain, with a short pause between each. Fathers have to guess their own son. Any fancy head-gear or tail should be removed first. Let the fathers then go behind the curtain, and Cubs do the guessing.

Fancy Dress Parade.

Meanwhile fathers help to string up apples.

Apples on String.

Equipment needed: apples
string

Apples are strung up on a beam, one side for boys and one for fathers.

Or:

Ducking for Apples.

Equipment needed: water
bowls
apples

Two large bowls of water—Cubs versus Dads. On signal of 'Go', number ones run up, link their arms behind their backs, and using only their teeth, try to remove an apple from the bowl.

Refreshments.

(*a*) Potatoes baked in their jackets, and kept warm in foil.

(*b*) Sausages on sticks.

(*c*) Drinks—'Dragons Blood' (perhaps home-made wine for Dads).
—'Witches Brew', which could be coloured lemonade for Cubs. (Bottles should be clearly labelled.)

Wicked Wizards.

Equipment needed: crêpe paper
newspaper
lining paper
pins and paper-clips
cardboard

Cubs dress up their fathers as Wizards.

A Grand Parade and prizes (apple or orange) is given to the best Wizard.

Conker King.

Equipment needed: conkers
string

A competition—Cubs versus fathers.

The Haunted House. (Kim's Game.)

Equipment needed: cassette recorder
tape recording of various sounds
pencils
paper

Cubs and fathers are scattered about the room. Lights are turned out. Everyone is told they are in a haunted house and must try to recognise various sounds without making any comment out loud. Sounds could be—creaking door, someone climbing the stairs, wind whistling round the house, door banging, cat mewing, etc. Light on—paper and pencil per Six. Make a list of sounds.

Camp Fire.

Outside round a wood fire would be ideal but, if indoors, an indoor fire of logs, red crêpe paper and torch. Candles in bottles round the 'fire'.

Opening—'Who hath smelt the woodsmoke.'

(Rudyard Kipling.)

The Witches Spell.

Equipment needed: caldron (perhaps a large stewing-pot)

A spell is read out, and various objects are brought out of the caldron, e.g. 'bat's blood' (tomato ketchup), 'frog's eye' (grape), 'dog's tongue' (banana skin), etc.

Three Little Ghostie Whosties

Three little ghostie whosties,
sitting on three postie whosties
eating buttered toasty whosties.
All the little greasty wheasties
running down their facety wasties.
Ah h h h h h! the dirty little beasty wheasties.
(a one-time Guide favourite)

Turnip Tops. *(The Second Gilwell Camp Fire Book)*. Both are now out of print, but maybe found in your Group Library.

Do not sing it, but all say the words and, on the word 'Late', clap hands to represent gun going off, and lay on backs with legs in the air.

Getty off them turnip tops.
Getty off that gate mate.
If you don't, I'll get my gun
and then it will be too *late* mate.

Read Act IV of Macbeth.

If Akela and her two Assistants can be dressed as the three witches, so much the better.

There was an Old Woman who swallowed a Fly.
(The Second Gilwell Camp Fire Book)

We're out for Gore. *(Gilwell Camp Fire Book)*

We're out for Gore
We're out for Gore—(*loud*)
We're out for Gore—(*very loud*)

(Make a noise of screwing a chicken's neck.)

BLOOD—(*shouted*).

Finish the Camp Fire with *Going Down the Valley.*
(The Scout Fire and Folk Song Book)

Boys change back into Cub uniform for an orderly finish of Grand Howl and Prayers.

HOME HELP BADGE.

This is usually a popular badge, so the poor Badge Examiner always has small invasions of boys. Why not try this idea:

Type out a list of requirements and give this to each parent, asking them to run through these with their own son, and write their comment on the result alongside each item.

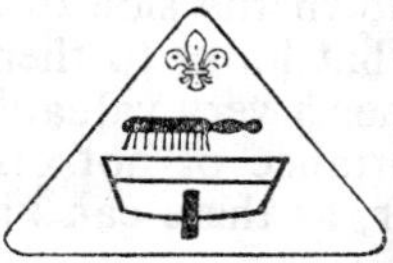

Get in touch with the Badge Examiner and invite her along to your headquarters to test the boys. Several Group Council members would, no doubt, come along to help test the boys. Set up the different requirements in a circle round your headquarters and give each Cub a card with the tests printed on it. Each requirement is signed as he passes. Aprons should be worn. Cubs bring their own food, plates, mugs and cutlery. This programme needs a good two hours, or can be divided up and spread over two weeks.

Sew on a badge or button.

Equipment: thread, needles, buttons, thick material to represent badges.

↓

Clean brass or silver.

Equipment: plenty of rags, horse brasses, cutlery, etc., polishes.

↓

Clean and tidy a room.

Equipment: brooms, brush and pan, dusters.

↓

Chips, bacon or sausage.

Equipment: small cooker, frying-pan, fat.

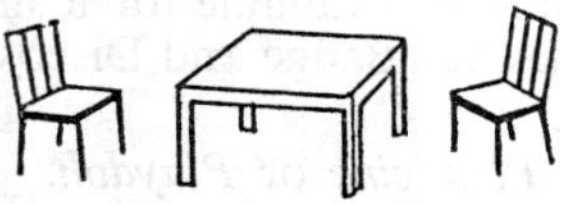

Lay a table and serve a meal.

Boil an egg.

Equipment: small cooker, saucepan, timer.

Lay a table and serve a meal.

↓

Make a bed.

Equipment: camp bed, lilo as mattress, sheets, pillow, blankets.

↓

Wash-up.

If no running-water and sink, bowls of water will be needed. Teacloths.

VISIT A FARM—Country Code **(Sharing).**

This will really bring home to the Cubs the importance of always shutting a gate, and if it will not open, then the correct way to climb over is always the hinge end. Also the importance of keeping to footpaths or walking down the side of a field and not through the middle. Even what looks to them like an ordinary field of grass is to the farmer a very valuable crop. The Cubs will also learn the importance of not discarding plastic bags when the picnic is over, as these can kill cattle.

HEALTH (Growing Up).

Collect together magazine and newspaper pictures of food—all kinds, e.g. ice-cream, roast beef, cream sponges, apples, sweets, butter, etc. Provide each Six with two large sheets of brown paper, one headed up 'Foods that are good for us', and the other 'Foods we should not eat too much of'. Then let them set to with the glue-pot.

ARROWS—group activities.

If you are short of help one evening, let the boys get into various activity groups for ten or 15 minutes on things they can work on without constant supervision.

Examples:

(*a*) One group of, say, four boys could be playing 'snap' with special bird-cards (obtainable from Guide Headquarters). Packs of wild flowers and wild animals are also available and could be used for another group.

(*b*) A group of older boys could make a scale model of a 250-foot hill using polystyrene tiles.

(*c*) Repairing books if you have a Pack library.

(*d*) Lego or something similar could be available for a small group to make a working model. (Artist Badge and Discovering).

(*e*) Modelling, using either clay, *Plasticine* or *Playdoh.*

(*f*) Tape recording of an expedition or a story.

TELEPHONE (Sharing).

'Show how to use a Directory and Code-Book.'

Give each Six a Directory, Code-Book and a 'Discovery Card'.

A 'Discovery Card' is just a postcard written as follows:

1. Write out the surname of each boy in your Six, then with the aid of the local directory, find out which is the most uncommon surname.
2. Find out the dialling codes of the following places . . . (List here ten places within a certain area.)

KNOW YOUR DISTRICT. (Sharing).

This Six activity is in some way linked with the above, but this time the Cubs use the Yellow Pages. Once again give each Six a 'Discovery Card' as follows:

A friend is coming to this district shortly.

1. Can you find the name, address and telephone number of a local hotel?
2. A garage where she can have her car repaired?
3. The name of a local Car-Hire firm?
4. The telephone number of the local National Westminster Bank?
5. The name and telephone number of a hairdresser?
6. The name and telephone number of a local dentist?
7. Finally, this friend has some valuable antiques she wishes to sell. Have you the name and address of a local antique dealer?

ART AND CRAFT.

Seed Collage—Cubs can create all sorts of designs and pictures, using a wide variety of seeds which are readily available, and not at all expensive. A useful book on the subject is *Introducing Seed Collage*, by Caryl and Gordon Simms (Batsford. 93 photographs.)

Wood—Ask your Cubs to look around in woods, parks or commons for pieces of wood that are lying about. The wood might be chosen for its unusual shape, its colour or maybe its texture.

The wood is then brought along to your next Pack Meeting where it is carefully sanded. Next, linseed oil is rubbed well in, and when this is dry, French Polish is rubbed on with a clean, soft rag.

Several pieces of wood could be put together to make a collage, or maybe a model of an animal or person. However, if any are of an interesting shape, they would make unusual ornaments.

Should you wish to go still further with your Pack, The National Federation of Women's Institutes have published a booklet entitled *Introduction to Simple Wood Sculpture*.

Polyfilla Pictures.

Equipment needed:
- small pieces of hardboard
- a large packet of *Polyfilla*
- small containers (soft margarine cartons are ideal)
- water
- rags
- newspaper for tables

plastic objects, i.e. toy soldiers, fish, animals, small wheels for patterns

Each Cub mixes the *Polyfilla* to a thick paste, and then smoothes it over his piece of hardboard. Plastic objects are placed in the mixture, and small toy car-wheels or buttons are used to make patterns. When the *Polyfilla* is dry, the pictures are sprayed with either copper or silver paint.

Rubbings—Send the Cubs out in their Sixes, armed with plenty of paper and thick wax crayons. Ask them to make rubbings of as wide a range of textured surfaces as they can find. Make a wall display of these rubbings. If you give

each Six wax crayons of their Six colour, you will be able to tell at a glance which Six has the most interesting collection. A word of warning; the Cubs should ask politely before making a rubbing of a doctor's brass-plate, and should never wander on to private property without seeking permission first.

Corn Dollies.

Should you decide to hold a Harvest Supper instead of the usual Pack Meeting around the end of September, the right decorations could make quite a difference.

Corn Dollies are something we would never have thought of tackling, but now, Hygienex Industries are producing 18-inch long **Artstraws.** With these, children of Cub age can produce excellent decorations and models. A pack of 2000 straws contains suggestions for their use. For further details write to Hygienex Industries Ltd., College Road, Fishponds, Bristol.

Polystyrene Tiles—These are not very expensive, and can be used for many activities with the Pack, i.e. outlines of witches and cats for a Hallowe'en Evening, relief models for the Map Reader badge, cut-out letters for display, mobiles, etc. *Arnolds* hot-wire polystyrene cutting tool is excellent for this. Write to E. J. Arnold & Son Ltd., Butterley Street, Leeds, LS10 1AX.

Macrame.

When the Cubs have mastered the reef knot and the round turn and two half-hitches, they can try their hand at Macramé. This is a technique which requires very little experience, and with just the knowledge of these two knots, it is possible to produce varied and interesting results. Cubs could make book-marks, and some of the older boys might like to try making belts and ties at Pack Meetings which could be finished at home. An excellent book on the subject is *Introducing Macramé*, by Eirian Short (B. T. Batsford Ltd.).

Copydex Adhesive.

Send to Copydex Ltd., Department AC10, 1 Torquay Street, London, W2 5BR, for their illustrated worksheets and teacher's notes for new handicraft ideas. Please enclose a large stamped addressed envelope.

(*a*) Tie and Dye and (*b*) Finart Fabricrayon.

(*a*) This is a well-established school activity which we would find difficult to do in the short time that is available at Pack Meetings. However, (*b*) *Finart* have brought out a unique crayon which is first used on paper, and then transferred to fabric with a warm iron. This opens up many possibilities for Cub activities. Write for information to Cosmic Crayon Company Ltd., Ampthill Road, Bedford.

Newclay.

This is clay with nylon reinforcement to make it non-brittle. It hardens as it dries, but additional hardness can be achieved by the use of a special hardener.

This type of clay can find a place in many of your Cub projects—modelling houses, bridges or ancient monuments for 'know your district' and 'local history'. **Newclay** over a ball of damp newspaper makes puppet heads for playacting, relief maps to help Cubs to understand map reading and contours, pottery and jewellery for Cub sales, etc.

Newclay is now available in most art and handcraft shops.

An average size Cub Pack will need at least a 28-lb. pack, and this is available at most art shops, in plastic tubs.

An excellent little book on *Newclay* is in the 'Starting Point' series of books published by Evans. It is number four and is entitled *Let's Model.* It is written by Alan Lewis This is a booklet that children can easily understand.

Brass-rubbings.

(*a*) This is an activity that can be brought into knowledge of your district, and also local history. Ask the priest's permission to make the rubbings, and only take a few boys at a time.

Equipment needed: roll of kitchen paper
sticks of heel-ball or
wax crayons
clean dusters
Sellotape

(*b*) As a follow-up of the above, or if your local church has no suitable brasses for rubbing, let the boys make their own.

Equipment needed: one piece of thick foil for each Cub
a drawing of a knight or lady in period costume done on greaseproof paper
Sellotape
pencils
black acrylic paint
paint-brushes
kitchen towel roll
newspaper

Each Cub places his drawing on to his foil, and *Sellotapes* it in place. He goes over every line with a pencil, pressing hard. When he is sure that he has finished, the *Sellotape* is carefully removed and the foil is turned over and placed on to a newspaper. Using a pencil, each Cub goes over every line of his drawing once again. The foil is then turned over and the black acrylic paint is brushed over the drawing with a thick brush. After a minute or two a clean piece of kitchen tissue is wiped once down the foil to give a good finish. Outlines can then be tidied up, and the picture carefully cut out and pasted on to a piece of black paper.

Winter

WINTER OUTINGS.

(*a*) The Cubs will love a visit to a cinema for a matinée performance. If the Pack is a large one, it is wise to give a warning to the Manager a few days before the intended visit. (*b*) Christmas holidays—After the Cubs have got over the rich foods of Christmas and visits to pantomimes, it would be an excellent idea to arrange a short hike or expedition. The weather is rarely so bad as to prevent this, and anyway snow would conjure up many different possibilities. However, it would, no doubt, be appreciated by Cubs and Scouters alike, if at one point a parent or friend could lay on hot cocoa or soup.

SNOW.

Should there be quite a bit of snow at one Pack Meeting, why not organise a special Pack Meeting of Winter Sports, with a Six activity of building the biggest and best Snowman.

FOLK DANCING.

This is becoming more and more popular among children, so why not introduce Folk Dancing or an occasional Square Dance to a Pack Meeting. If you need any advice or help with suitable dances, write to The English Folk Dance and Song Society, Cecil Sharp House, 2 Regent's Park Road, N.W.1, who will, no doubt, put you into touch with the Secretary of your local group. Folk Dancing is something that will always go down well at a Parents' Evening.

PACK GOOD TURN.

If you haven't yet introduced your Cubs to knitting, you should certainly do so. Why not a knitted blanket of many-coloured squares to be presented to an old lady living nearby, or an Old People's Home? Mothers will enjoy helping their sons, and are bound to find numerous odd balls of wool in their work-baskets. After one or two sessions at Pack Meetings, squares can be knitted at home, and the finished product brought along each week when Scouters can give points, say 10 points plus a bonus for a really excellent square. It is wise to state what size square you want and what ply wool to use, otherwise there will be difficulty in the sewing-up stage.

BOOK READER.

(*a*) Provided that you have adequate cupboard space, why not start your own Cub Library? The boys should be asked to bring along any books in good condition that are no longer required, and any of your friends with children might also help as well. The Sixers and Seconds may well spend an additional evening helping you to number and list the books as they come in. When all the preparations are completed, appoint two librarians for the month and open the library for 10 minutes before Pack Meetings.

(*b*) Having your own Cub library will give the boys a chance to make some book covers. Come along to your Pack Meeting armed with plenty of brown paper, crayons, etc., and before setting the Cubs to work, give a demonstration yourself. When the books are nicely covered, get the boys to print the title carefully and perhaps draw and crayon an appropriate picture on the front.

(*c*) Ask your local Librarian if you may bring a party of

Cubs to his library. They will be told how the Library operates, and shown the way to repair books and the proper way to treat them. The Cubs would then be able to repair the books in their Cub Library.

SEA SHELLS.

Ask the Cubs to make a collection of sea-shells when they go to the coast, and then hold a Special Pack Meeting in the winter. Choose a King Neptune, and ask the rest of the Cubs to make an appropriate costume, i.e. mermen, seaweed, fish, etc. Decorate your headquarters to represent the sea—

green crêpe paper cut into strips and pulled to look like sea-weed. Large cut-outs of fish, star-fish and shells can be hung from the ceiling and pinned on the walls. Have suitable games and activities: the old favourites 'The Sea is very Rough today' is a very good one. With the aid of shells, pipe-cleaners and modelling clay, each Six could make an animal or arrange a decoration and then paint or varnish the finished article.

A useful book is *Undersea Craft*, by M. C. Green and B. R. H. Targett and published by Harrap.

CHRISTMAS DECORATIONS.

Run a Christmas Decoration Competition. Tell the Cubs about this at the beginning of December to give them plenty of time to think something up. These can be put up by the boys and Scouters before the last Meeting when a local person is asked if he or she will come along to do the judging.

PLASTICINE.

Give each Six a few sticks of plasticine and ask them to make a Cub Trophy. Provide small wooden bases to add the finishing touch.

SCRAPBOOK OF EVENTS.

Each week, one boy in a Six is responsible for collecting and pasting into a scrapbook important and interesting daily events. Competition for the best scrapbook. It is best to set a certain time limit.

HERALDRY.

Explain to the Pack how knights of old each had their own Coat-of-Arms. Cut out a cardboard shield and make your own Coat-of-Arms to show your boys, and then tell them they will be making their own next week. They might wish to bring the appropriate cut out pictures if they are young Cubs and not very good at drawing. Scouters should make the shields for the boys. When finished, the Cubs can fix the shields to the wall in their Six corners, or maybe take them home for their bedroom wall. Give the Cubs plenty of ideas for filling the four sections, i.e. Arrows, Sixer or Second stripes, hobbies, sports, Cub Badges gained, County Badge, pictures of farm animals or a tractor if living on a farm, school badge, nationality, surname, etc.

HOME HELP.

(*a*) Not many boys know the correct way to lay a table, so why not make a set of cardboard plates, knives, forks, spoons, glasses, etc., or set the boys to make them. They will be wonderful for instruction and even a relay game.

(*b*) Brass Cleaning—No doubt most of you have quite a collection of horse brasses and various other ornaments of this type, so why not take them along to a Pack Meeting together with cleaning liquid and rags, and hold a Six Competition for the ornaments with the most shine. It might be worth adding that any mess on clothes looses a point.

EXPLORING (Sharing).

(*a*) Draw a large map of the British Isles, and pin it up in your headquarters. Ask the Cubs to collect as many different

postmarks as they can find, and on arrival at the Pack Meeting or at any spare moment let them stick their own on the correct places. Have an Atlas or two on hand. Do not let this run on too long, but give a set time; perhaps a month.

(*b*) Ask parents if they will let you have any old A.A. Handbooks. One per Six is ideal. Armed with these, give each Six a town about 30 miles away and ask them to use their book to plan the quickest route from your headquarters. Once they have reached their town, ask them to find out the population of the town together with early closing day and the last post.

You will, no doubt find many other uses for the A.A. Handbook, but one activity which the Cubs will enjoy is to collect car numbers, and then to look them up in the Handbook to find out where they come from.

ST. ANDREW'S NIGHT.

If your Pack Meeting happens to fall on 30th November, do take the opportunity of having a St. Andrew's Night. It

need not be very elaborate, but you can be sure that the boys will be more likely to remember the date and about St. Andrew than just sitting listening to an instruction session. Have a knotting game on mending the fishing-nets: let your yarn be about the five loaves and two fishes, suitably illustrated. If your Pack funds can stand it, why not buy or make some shortbread to give to the boys at the end of your Meeting.

SKY AT NIGHT.

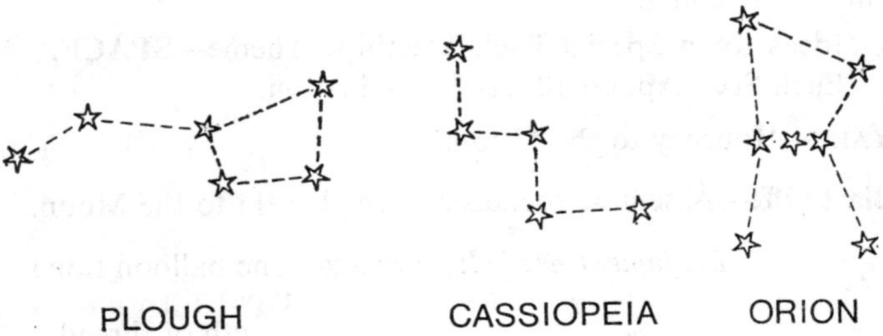

Pack Activities.

(*a*) Star charts for wall decoration.

Equipment needed: black paper
silver stars

Boys working on this Arrow requirement could make small charts to put into their log-books, or large charts for instruction.

(*b*) Star observation.

Equipment needed: empty yoghurt cartons
black paper
glue
pins
torches

Remove the bottom of several yoghurt cartons very carefully. Place the top of the cartons on to the black paper and draw as many circles as you have cartons. Cut these out and then prick a different constellation on each circle. Stick the circles on to the cartons. Now, armed with your torches, take the Pack outside.

(*c*) YARNS—*Legends of the Stars*, by Patrick Moore (Odhams Books Ltd.).

Read one story each week, and use the star charts for illustration. Or, if you prefer, use a record.

(*d*) Play-acting—Any of the Legends. If these are done in costume they would make wonderful entertainment for a Parents' Evening.

Ideas for a Special Pack Meeting—Theme—**SPACE.**
Each Six—Apollo 10–11–12, and so on.

YARN—'Journey to the Moon.'

Blast Off!—Assemble rockets and send them to the Moon.

Equipment needed: per Six—one balloon (long type)
length of thread
Sellotape
drinking-straw

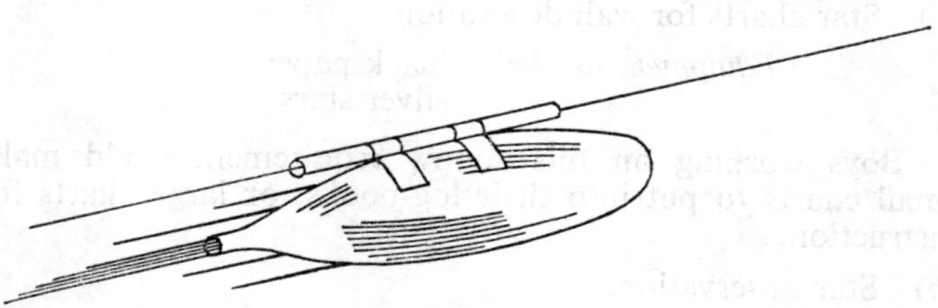

Tape drinking-straw to the balloon. Pass the thread through the straw, and fix one end round a beam.

Each Six blows up their balloon and holds the end tightly. everyone waits—5—4—3—2—1—BLAST OFF. Let go of the balloons. First to reach the target is the winner.

Circle the Moon.

Equipment needed: four treacle tins with a loop of string in each one

Circle of Cubs who represent the Moon.

One Cub runs round the circle holding a pair of tins on each arm. He stands one pair of tins behind a Cub; they then both mount their tins, and go in opposite directions round the circle and back through the opening to the centre of the circle where 'Smarties' (space food) are in the space-ship (a bucket or similar).

Space Helmet. Pack activity. (Simple Handcraft.)

Equipment needed: large paper bags
cardboard
paper-clips, etc.

'Smarties' for the best helmet.

Building a Station on the Moon.

Equipment needed: bean-bag per Six

Pack form a wheel-shape in their Sixes.

Centre boy passes the bean-bag out to the boy on the end of his Six, who runs round and back to the centre. The Six moves out, and so on.

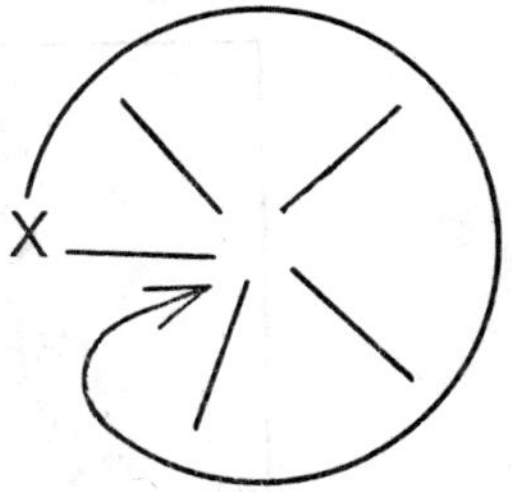

Communication with Moon Beings!

Relay formation—Play Acting—Mime.

Cubs run up in order, then go back to their Six to act one of the following in mime:

I would like something to eat.
We live in things called houses.
Our favourite sport is football.
I am tired, where can I go to bed?
I am from another world.
I am very cold, etc.

Moon—Mars.

Equipment needed: none

Cubs are scattered about the room.
'Moon'—All run to the top of the room.
'Mars'—All run to the bottom of the room.
Blast Off—Lie flat on backs.
Meteorites—Roll up into a ball.
Martians—Scatter to the sides of the room.

Make a Model of a Space Craft. (Simple Handicraft.)

Equipment needed: toilet-roll tubes
squeezy bottles
Plasticine
lolly-sticks
scissors and anything to hand

COLLECTION.

Ask all the boys to empty out their pockets.

Which Six has (*a*) the most useful.

(*b*) the most interesting or unusual,

(*c*) the most varied collection.

CHRISTMAS GIFTS.

Cubs make calendars, using old Christmas cards, bits of ribbons, etc. Then organise a Carol Evening (well rehearsed), and visit the homes of old people. Instead of accepting money, give a calendar.

CUB SCOUT, BROWNIE GUIDE, GUIDE AND SCOUT CHRISTMAS GOOD TURN.

At the beginning of December, hold a party for the 65's and over in your area. Send out invitation letters, which can be delivered by Cubs and Brownies and, if your Group funds can stand it, a stamped addressed envelope should be attached. Ask the Committee members to organise the transport.

The programme could go as follows:

The Guides prepare tea and lay the tables, maybe with a pretty centre-piece.

Tea—served by the Sixers and Seconds of the Packs.

A short Carol Service with readings by the Cubs and Brownies. This is followed by the clergyman blessing the presents around the tree.

Presents handed to guests by the children.

Nativity play by the Guides and Scouts.

There will, no doubt, be quite a number of old people who were unable to come to the party. Perhaps the Scouts could deliver a small present to each one.

A party which finishes before dark would be more acceptable to old people.

VISITORS (Thinking).

Boys often like a change of face, so why not occasionally invite someone along to talk to them for 20 minutes in place of your yarn, i.e. Policeman, Postman, a Fireman, an R.S.P.C.A. or Dr. Barnardo representative, etc. If you invite a policeman to your meeting, the games sessions could be on this theme. For example—observation, a Z-cars game, prisoners, etc.

You might like to have a month of collecting silver paper

to give to the R.S.P.C.A. representative when he comes, or collect toys in good condition for Dr. Barnardo's Homes.

CAROL SERVICE.

Ask the Vicar's permission to hold a short Carol Service in the Church one Pack Meeting before Christmas. Send out invitations to parents and friends, and all the boys on the waiting-list and their parents. If you only have a small Pack, why not join up with the Brownies for that evening?

HOBBY HORSES.

With old socks or stockings, stuffing, wool, buttons and a collection of sticks, let the boys make their own hobby horses and hold races. These horses could be used for a Special Pack Meeting or for display at a Parents' Evening.

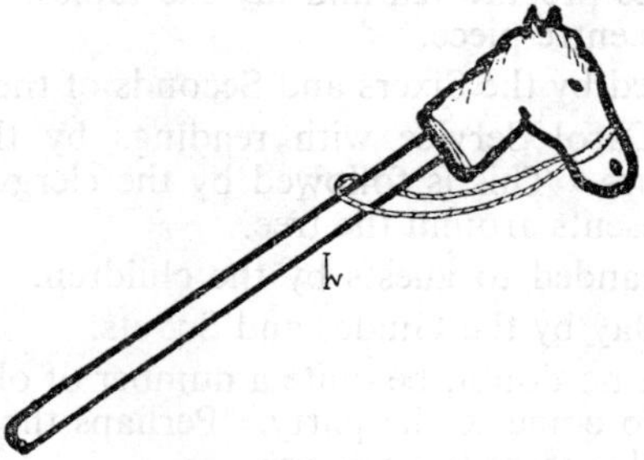

HOBBIES MONTH.

Encourage the boys to talk about their hobbies, and bring their collections along to the Pack Meetings.

Look among parents, committee members and friends, and maybe you will find someone with an unusual hobby, and another with a hobby most popular with your boys, and so on. Each week of the month, invite one of these people along, and work your programme around each hobby.

SUGGESTIONS:

(*a*) A member of the local football or cricket team (Sportsman Badge). Have a sports evening, with perhaps each Six representing their favourite team and sporting their colours. Run short matches of five-a-side football, and have a sports quiz.

(*b*) **A Numismatist.**

Ask any keen Cub coin collectors to bring their collection to the Pack Meeting. Games and activities could include coin rubbing, roll a penny, etc.

(*c*) **A Taxidermist.**

He might like a fresh body of a bird that has just been knocked over by a car, or a mole perhaps!

(*d*) **An Amateur Photographer.**

Ask the Cubs to mount and label any of their photographs they particularly like, and hold a photographic exhibition.

(*e*) **A Mother Who Enjoys Cooking.**

A demonstration of quick cooking and sweetmaking, with the Cubs trying their hand afterwards.

(*f*) **A Keen Bird Watcher.**

A slide show on birds in your area.

SPECIAL PACK MEETING—Z CARS.

Visitor—local policeman.

Boys have been asked the previous week to bring along any model cars they may have.

Inspection—General smartness.

Stop—get ready—Go.

Equipment needed: three cardboard discs about 12 inches in diameter, coloured red, amber and green

When Akela holds up green disc—all rush about the room,
amber disc—touch any wall and keep still,
red disc—freeze.

Z-Cars.

Equipment needed:—a prepared story

Each Six in relay formation and representing a Patrol Car—Z victor 1, Z victor 2, and so on.

Tell a yarn about jewel thieves; bring in the following phrases:

(*a*) Catch the robbers—running relay;
(*b*) Piece together clue No. 1—a message cut into pieces, collected in relay and put together;
(*c*) Patrolling streets—walking relay;
(*d*) Police dogs—relay on all fours;
(*e*) Decode second clue—compass drawing. (Using graph paper, draw a picture using compass directions.)

Six Activity.

Equipment needed: large sheets of brown paper or lining paper
Plasticine
lolly-sticks
crayons or chalk
boxes

Each Six is given paper and chalk, etc. They mark out roads, roundabouts, etc., make road signs using card, lolly-sticks and plasticine; and set out their cars. Visitor inspects each Six's efforts and gives comments.

BADGES.

Many Scouters say that they never find the time to touch on badges at a Pack Meeting, so they just concentrate on the Arrow requirements. But having a particular badge as your monthly theme does not mean that Arrow requirements and games are left out. Also, using a badge as the theme for the whole Pack could introduce a boy to a hobby or interest he might otherwise never have thought of taking up.

ENTERTAINER BADGE.

Simple mimes and acting games play a great part in our programmes and help our Cubs to learn many things they would otherwise perhaps find difficult.

Ideas for using the Entertainer Badge as your monthly theme:

(*a*) **Build a Puppet Theatre.** (Simple handcrafts.)

Give each Six two or three potatoes, small pieces of material, wool, pins, paper bags, etc., and tell them that they have 20 minutes to make some puppets and to plan a short sketch. An Instructor can help with hollowing out the neck of the potatoes and making the faces. Instead of potatoes, yoghurt cartons scrubbed clean make excellent heads for puppets.

The stage can be a small table covered by a cloth large enough to touch the floor, and two chairs laid face down with backs just touching each other. The legs of the chairs can be covered and a black cloth added. A torch at each corner of the stage makes very good footlights. Boys love this form of play acting and it gives a wonderful chance for the shy Cub to come into his own, as he can be heard but not seen.

(*b*) A puppet theatre can be made with several giant-sized

Cornflakes packets glued together and covered with brown paper.

Boys who are working for the Scientist badge could make stage lighting with bulbs and batteries. Instructions for this are in the Ladybird book *Magnets, Bulbs and Batteries.*

(*c*) A large egg-box from a grocer would make an excellent puppet theatre for string puppets. Scenery could be painted by the Cubs on large sheets of paper and, at the change of the scene, the new scenery could be let down through a slit in the top of the box.

Costume.

Most Packs will have their own dressing-up box. If not, why not go along to your next local jumble sale. It is surprising what use can be made of old sheets and curtains.

Activity.

Tell each Six that the costumes are missing, and that they have 10 minutes to create one from the odds and ends in a sack. Give each Six a card with the character to be copied, i.e. a Roman Soldier, Dougal from B.B.C. Television's Magic Roundabout, Long John Silver, etc. Make sure that the odds and ends you have in the sack are in keeping with the characters you choose.

Make-up.

Most towns and villages have Amateur Dramatic Societies. Why not ask if one of their number would come along to a Pack Meeting and tell the boys about make-up, and maybe show them how to change the shape of the nose, age a person, make a face appear thinner or fatter, put on false whiskers and bushy eyebrows, etc.

Wigs. Pack Activity.

Equipment needed: thick wool (hair colour)
balloons
nylon stockings
tape

Blow up the balloon to the size of the head. Tie a knot in the top of the nylon stocking, then cut the stocking several inches below this knot and stretch it over the balloon. Secure this with *Sellotape* to stop it from slipping off. Now start sticking pieces of wool on to a long strip of tape. When this has been done, arrange the tape, sticking as you go, round and round the balloon head. Many styles can be created in this way.

Sound Effects.

Everyone knows that two halves of a coconut shell beating on a tray of gravel sound like horses hooves.

A short radio sketch can be performed, bringing in as many sounds as possible, and also any appropriate music.

(*a*) Rain—crumpled paper and rice. Pick up two handfuls of rice and let it drop on to the paper.

(*b*) Thunder—a sheet of tin.

(*c*) A creaking stair or door—a small barrel, string, cloth and resin. Thread the string through the top of the barrel and tie a knot in the end. Put a little resin on to the cloth and pull up the length of the string with it. The creak will alter in sound as you move up the string.

(*d*) Someone walking up the garden path—put some gravel in an empty cereal box and seal with brown paper. Tip from hand to hand for the sound of feet.

Mime and Music.

Play different types of music at a Pack Meeting and ask the Cubs to do whatever the music suggests to them.

Lead the Pack in some form of Folk Dancing.

Some boys will do Folk Dancing at school, and, therefore, will be full of suggestions for various dances. Let them go ahead and teach the Pack. If this is new to both you and the Cubs, then get into touch with your local Folk Dance Society and ask for their help with instruction and records. If you do not know where the nearest group is, write to The English Folk Dance Society, Cecil Sharp House, 2 Regent's Park Road, London, N.W.1., and they will put you in touch with your nearest group. Folk Dancing also makes a very good display for a Parents' Evening.

AN UNUSUAL GIFT.

Tell your Cubs that you are going to give each Six an unusual gift and that you want to know how they will react to it. They are given about five minutes to prepare a short scene. Gifts could be £1,000, a dirty plate, a baby fox, an aeroplane, etc. The cleverest and most original wins.

HOT NEWS.

Equipment needed: a daily newspaper per Six.

Give each Six a newspaper and let them have a certain time to choose a story. Then act it before the rest of the Pack.

CASSETTE RECORDER.

No doubt many of you are now using a cassette recorder for some of your Pack activities. It is particularly helpful for the Entertainer Badge because it can be used to simulate radio plays, is ideal for story telling, and can be used to produce sound effects when required.

DYES.

Use natural dyes on pieces of old sheeting to create different costumes, i.e. beetroot, strong coffee, leaves, etc.

Soak the beetroot, leaves, berries, etc., overnight and next day bring to the boil and strain. Dip your material into this.

MUSICAL INSTRUMENT RELAY.

Equipment needed: none

Number one from each Six runs up to Akela and is given a musical instrument to mime, i.e. triangle, drum, violin, harp, piano, recorder, etc.

THE JUNGLE.

Equipment needed: none

Cubs are scattered about the room. Akela calls out an animal. The boy who makes the most realistic animal gains a point for his Six.

MIME.

Some boys are shy of taking speaking parts, but given a set thing to do in mime, they really enjoy it.

Give each Six a written list of three actions and let them have a certain time for preparation. Each Six must try to guess what the other's actions are, i.e. (*a*) Take a nasty dose of medicine; (*b*) You are a shop assistant selling shoes to a customer with big feet; (*c*) Indicate to your Doctor that you have a pain in your back owing to too much gardening; (*d*) Ring your dentist and make an appointment to have a tooth pulled; (*e*) You are a barber.

CHRISTMAS MIME.

On the last Pack Meeting before Christmas ask each Six to act a Carol in mime.

PERFORM THREE CONJURING TRICKS.

Give each Six a printed postcard with instructions written on it for a trick. Also give them any equipment they may need. Ideas for tricks can be obtained from The Ladybird *Book of Magic*. Let each Six perform their trick in front of the rest of the Pack.

BADGE EXAMINER.

If the Pack are going to do some entertaining at your Parents' Evening, invite the Entertainer Badge Examiner along. Do not forget to give him a programme and a list of boys' names.

COOKING IN THE PACK.

Cooking.

Cubs love being given the opportunity to cook, but even today there are still parents who believe in keeping their children out of the kitchen, and you will, no doubt, find boys in your Pack who are never allowed to try their hand at cooking at home.

Of course, many Packs have sausage sizzles out of doors in summer months, but what about winter months at Pack Meetings? Look out for advertisements of second-hand '*Baby Belling*' cookers. These can easily be carried around in the back of a Scouter's car. Perhaps you could insert a 'Wanted' advertisement in your Group magazine or in a letter to the parents. Also most Scout Troops have calor gas stoves that you might be able to borrow.

A few cooking ideas:

Christmas Cooking.

Each Six makes one of the following:

Mince pies
Sausage rolls
Peppermint Creams
Chocolate truffles
Fudge

A Scouter or Cub mother should be in charge of each group.

Candle Cooking.

If the Pack have no cooker, why not try cooking this way. First find as many large tins as you can. Tins used for baby milk powder are ideal. Punch a few holes in the tins, then turn them upside down over lighted candles (stand the candles in baking tins). You now have your cooking stove. Make your dough by mixing flour, baking-powder, and sugar with a little water. Make the little dough cakes on the top of your 'cooker', but don't forget to grease the top first.

Toffee Apples.

The recipe can be found in any cookery book. These can be sold at your Pack Bring-and-Buy Sale.

Pancakes—Shrove Tuesday.

These are always popular. *See* Page 24 under 'Spring'.

A Pack Harvest Supper.

(*a*) The Cubs cook the meal at the Pack Meeting.

Perhaps: one Six prepare and cook the potatoes;
one Six prick and cook the sausages;
one Six mix the soup.

Each boy cores his own apple, and then queues for the fruit for stuffing and the brown sugar.

Whilst the meal is cooking, Cubs set out the tables, lay the cloths and set their places.

(*b*) Have a general discussion to decide on the Menu for your Harvest Supper. When this is done, let each Six be responsible for each item, i.e. White Six—Shepherd's pie; Blue Six—Apple pie; Red Six—Custard; Yellow Six—Cocoa, and so on. This food is prepared at home and brought along to the Pack Meeting.

Cookery Competition.

When it comes to cake decoration and the finishing touches, boys easily beat the girls.

Try running a tea-time cooking competition to be done at home, with mother's full permission, and brought to the next Pack Meeting. Place a pretty tablecloth on the table and write out 1st, 2nd and 3rd prize cards. Invite along a member of the Group Executive Committee to do the judging, and without doubt she will have a difficult job choosing the winning entry, as there are sure to be quite a collection of fairy cakes, sponges, scones, girdle scones, etc.

International

INTERNATIONAL IDEAS.

It has been found, especially with rural Packs that the boys tend to think of themselves as just one small group. District events help them to realise that there are a great deal more Cubs in the neighbourhood, and if you can take them to an Adventure Day at County level where they are one of many thousands of Cub Scouts, get them to see how many different County Badges they can spot on Cub jerseys.

From there go on to World Cub Scouting. Draw a large map of the World and pin it on the wall of your headquarters, and then with the help from libraries, pen-friends, friends holidaying abroad, find out what you can about foreign Cubs and their activities. Every month or every two months adopt a country: say France is your first choice, get the Pack artist to draw a French Cub, and then stick him on the correct place on your map. Give the Cub a name and discuss what foods he eats, the type of school he attends, the various customs of his country, etc., and bring these into games and activities each week. For the last Pack Meeting of the month, ask the boys to bring anything French they have from home, and put them on display. You might be lucky enough to know a French person who would be willing to come along and talk to the boys. The French Embassy would also be able to help you.

There are many exciting possibilities if you can get a link with a Pack abroad. Maybe a tape correspondence could be started, and the highlights of your meetings taped and exchanged. The Scouters could exchange games and even whole programmes.

The following are some sample programmes:

DUTCH EVENING.

Visitor for the evening—a Dutchman.

Dutch Flag—on loan from the Dutch Embassy.

Headquarters—decorated with posters and drawings.

Display Table—anything Dutch brought by Cubs, plus models made at a previous Pack Meeting.

Grand Howl—as Cubs in Holland do it:

AKELA Wij – ij – ij doe – oe – oen o – o – ons best!

Dyb, Dyb, Dyb, Dyb.

Wij Dob – Dob – Dob – Dob, WOEF.

Inspection. Station in Holland (a Scouter at each Station).

Den Hague—caps and hair.

Amsterdam—nails and hands.

Rotterdam—uniform.

Arnhem—knees and shoes.

Clogs.

Equipment needed: pieces of string
two pieces of wood or corrugated cardboard stapled together (enough for each Cub)

Cubs make their clogs and then run a relay.

Windmills.

Equipment needed: none

One boy is the cat; one boy is the mouse. The rest of the Pack represent windmills and stand in rows in their Sixes, facing the top of the room which is north, arms outstretched sideways and holding their neighbour's hand. On the word

'Go', the cat chases the mouse away from the sacks of corn in and out of the windmills. When 'The wind blows west' is called, the windmills drop hands, turn left and hold hands with new neighbour. When the mouse is caught, a new cat and mouse are chosen.

Six Activity.

Each Six to make a Dutch scene from *Plasticine*, pipe cleaners, cocktail sticks, cardboard, etc.

e.g. Bridge over canal, the cheese market, etc.

Dutch Tour.

The Cubs are scattered about the room.
Windmills—swing arms round and round.
Skates—hands behind back and skating motion.
Sluice gates open—run to right side of the room.
Sluice gates closed—run to the left side of the room.
Amsterdam—run to the top of the room.
Rotterdam—run to the bottom of the room.
Bicycles—on backs, legs in air, with cycling motion.
Tulips—stand still, arms in air.

Refreshments.

Lemonade, Dutch cheese and biscuits.

Tape can be played at this time, or perhaps a letter read from Dutch link.

Activity.

Equipment needed: newspaper
paper-clips
coloured sticky paper

Each Cub makes a Dutch-type hat.

Dutch visitor talks to the Cubs about his country and answers any of their questions.

Tunnels and Bridges.

Equipment needed: none

Tunnels—relay formation. Last boy crawls through legs of Six, runs to the top of the room and then back to the front of his Six and so on.

Bridges—relay formation. Last boy clambers over the backs of his Six (who kneel down), runs to the top of the room, and then back to the front of his Six, and so on.

Grand Howl—as Dutch Cubs do it.

Flag down, followed by a suitable prayer.

HOLLAND is a good European country with which to have a Pack link-up, as most adults speak good English. If, however, you send over a tape try to get a native of that country to introduce your taped programme and to give a commentary throughout, as the majority of Dutch Cubs will not understand English.

Your first tape could start off with a description of your part of the country, your town or village, your headquarters, etc. Let your Sixers learn a few words of greeting, and why not learn a greeting yourself, and perhaps try an explanation of a game. Future tapes can tell of Pack Holidays and Pack Outings. Another could be solely entertainment. A letter tape can be purchased from any record shop.

AN AUSTRALIAN EVENING.

See if you can find an Australian willing to come along and join you for the evening.

Preparation—*Display Table*—Boys are asked the previous week to bring along anything typically Australian.

Pictures—also posters to decorate the walls of the headquarters. Try to obtain an Australian flag.

Grand Howl.

Australian Quiz.

Equipment needed: large map of Australia to pin on the wall

Sixes in relay formation—Scouter asks a question and calls a number. Boy runs and refers to the map, then runs to Scouter with the answer.

e.g. (*a*) States of Brisbane, Sydney, etc.
(*b*) Name an island.
(*c*) Where is Alice Springs?

Play Acting—Theme—Aborigines.

Equipment needed: Cub prop box

Sheep Shearing.

Equipment needed: none

Two teams of 'sheep shearers' (one half of the Pack). Rest of the Pack, who have on their outdoor coats, are sheep. Same number of sheep per team. On word 'Go' number one of each team runs up and shears first sheep (takes off cap, coat and scarf), and runs back to touch off next sheep shearer.

Six Activity.

(*a*) Draw and colour the flag of Australia.
(*b*) Make a boomerang from thick cardboard.

(*c*) Draw the outline of Australia.
(*d*) Draw a native animal of Australia.

Yarn—The Flying Doctor.

Bush Fires.

To an Australian Cub, knowing how to put out a fire effectively and also the precautions necessary for preventing fire, are very important.

Equipment needed: two cups of water per Six
one spoon per Six

Two cups of water, one at either end of each Six. The one at the back is filled with water. The end boy has a spoon, and on the word 'Fire', dips the spoon in the cup and hands the full spoon to the next boy, who in turn passes it on. When it reaches his Sixer he empties the water from the spoon into the cup at his end. The game continues until the cup at the back of the Six is empty. The first Six with the most water in the top cup is the winner.

Kangaroo Jump.

Equipment needed: none

Pack in Sixes. The first Cub makes the biggest jump he can—second Cub runs up to him and then jumps, third Cub runs to second Cub and jumps and so on. The Six with the longest jump wins.

Sing-Song.

Songs could include—*Waltzing Matilda, Kookaburra,* and several of the Rolf Harris favourites.

Grand Howl, Flag Down and Prayers.

Programmes.

Why not swop programmes? Perhaps a B.-P. Birthday Programme with an Australian Pack, one being held in bitterly cold wintry weather, the other taking place on a beach in a heatwave!

AMERICAN EVENING.

Held near American Independence Day.

Preparation—*Table for Exhibits* (brought by Cubs).

American flag if possible.

Each Six becomes Den 1, Den 2, Den 3, Den 4, etc.

Opening Ceremony—Each Den to give a Yell.

The following were sent over by a Den Mother:

(1) Grand Salute.
(count 1—2—3—4—5—)
Strike knees with hands five times
Stamp feet five times
Clap hands five times
Stand and Salute.

(2) D—Y—B, D—Y—B.
Happy, fair and game.
You do your best
and we'll do the same.

(3) Chase 'em down the valley
Run 'em down the street
Den No. 3 won't retreat.

(4) Rip 'em up, scratch 'em up
Tear 'em up and eat 'em.
You can't beat 'em
Y—e—o—w!

Here are some games American Cub Scouts play:

A Glider Contest.

Equipment needed: one piece of paper per boy, approximately 10″ × 12″
one paper-clip per boy
tape measure

Each boy makes a glider and, from a starting line, a test flight is made for the longest distance.

Den Activity.

Short word on F.B.I.

Each Den to make a file of their finger-prints.

Equipment needed: pencils
paper
Sellotape

Each boy rubs a piece of scrap paper with the side of his pencil, then rubs his finger on this mark. Cut an inch-strip of *Sellotape*, and press finger on to sticky side of the tape. Carefully remove and press tape on to clean sheet of paper. This way there is no spoiling the print. Papers can be hung up in Den corners.

Feathers on a Plate.

Equipment needed: one plate per Den
six feathers per Den

Relay game—Any feather dropped must be picked up.

Fifty-yard Swim.

Equipment needed: mug of water per Den

Relay game—Number one hops on one foot with mug of water to a line a short distance in front of each Den. He runs back, hands mug of water to number two who does the same. Den with most water left are the winners.

Bean Race.

Equipment needed: dried beans
lolly-sticks

Relay game—Place a pile of beans in front of each Den. Number one carries one bean between lolly-sticks to place in a cap some yards ahead. Then runs and touches off number two.

Closing Ceremony.

The American Cub Scout Law:

The Cub Scout follows Akela
The Cub Scout helps the Pack go,
The Pack helps the Cub Scout grow.
The Cub Scout gives good-will.

Before trying out this programme with your Pack, find out all you can about American Scouting and the American boy. Perhaps you will be lucky enough to start up correspondence with the Den Mother or the Akela.

IDEAS FOR AN INTERNATIONAL PACK EVENING

Special Pack Meeting.

Boys choose any country they like, and wear costume.
Grand Howl—maybe the French or Dutch way.
Inspection—finger-nails.

AUSTRALIA.

The Cane Cutter's Relay.

Equipment needed: one large rolled-up newspaper per Six
one chair per Six

Sixes in relay formation. Place one chair with rolled up newspaper on it some distance in front of each Six. On word 'go', number one runs to chair, grabs cane-knife (newspaper) and runs to the head of his Six. He then sweeps the floor with 'knife' (Six has to jump over to avoid knife), and on reaching the end of his Six, number one turns and lops off the top of the cane (Cubs drop on hands and knees to avoid being hit on the head with cane-knife). The cane-knife is then replaced on the chair, and number two repeats the performance. The last Cub replaces the cane-knife on to the chair and returns to his place at alert. First to finish wins.

JAPAN.

Six Activity—Handicraft.

Japanese lanterns or paper folding.

CANADA.

Shoot the Rapids.

Equipment needed: none

Cubs find a partner, and form a circle. One boy forms the inner circle and one forms the outside circle, standing directly behind his partner. Inside circle always stand still.

On the call of—'Shoot the rapids'—outside Cubs run clockwise in and out of Cubs standing still.

'Indians'—Make Indian noise whilst carrying on with any previous call.

'Logs approaching'—run in anti-clockwise direction.

'Change boats'—keep running in same direction until partner is reached, then go under his legs.

Last couple are out. You now have a new outside circle.

INDIA.

Some form of Kim's Game.

NEW ZEALAND.

A Simple Maori Stick Dance.

CHINA.

Chinese Writing.

Equipment needed: paper and pencils

Explain to the Pack about Chinese writing going up and down the page instead of from left to right like ours, and then ask each Six to produce a picture-story. Perhaps a nursery rhyme would be easy to begin with.

Refreshments—Ask each boy to bring some food from whichever country he is representing that evening.

Grand Howl, Flag Down and Prayers.

A PARENTS' EVENING WITH AN INTERNATIONAL THEME.

Why not give your Parents' Evening an International theme?

Arrange several tables round the room displaying the various materials you have used on your special evenings throughout the year. Maybe the Cubs made and painted some boomerangs on your Australian evening, or made or drew windmills on a Dutch evening. Collect colourful pictures of the countries and let the boys paste them on large sheets of paper for wall display. If you have refreshments, make out a few simple recipes of cakes, scones, biscuits, etc., of all the countries represented that evening, and enlist the help of the Cub mothers.

Put on a display of play-acting or even a demonstration of foreign games and then, after refreshments, you may have some slides to show of your Link, or maybe you could hire a film about another country or play some of your tapes.

The following is an example of play-acting for an International Evening for parents:

SCENE OPENS—*Outside curtains.*

CUB SCOUTER, SIXER and NEW BOY *sitting in spotlight.*

CUB SCOUTER—Well, Paul, you have been with the Pack for three weeks, and among other things you have learnt the Cub Promise, the Cub Law, the Salute and the Grand Howl. Tonight, for the first time you are wearing the Cub Scout uniform minus, of course, at present, the Group scarf and enrolment badges. Within the next hour you will become one of a big brotherhood. It goes all over the world. There are your brother Cubs everywhere—in Australia, Canada,

India, America, France, and in so many places that it is impossible to mention them all. The games they play and the tests they pass are adapted according to the climate in which they live, and although most Packs still have the Jungle as their background, there are a few whose methods are slightly different. Now Andrew, as you are Paul's Sixer, I will leave you to run over the ceremony again with him.

ANDREW—All right Akela. (AKELA *exits.*)

PAUL—I wish I could meet some of those Cubs; what fun it would be.

ANDREW—You'll get your chance one day; perhaps when you are a Scout and are chosen to go to a Jamboree.

PAUL—*That's* no good, I want to see them all now. Oh, I wish it were possible.

(*Suddenly a small light—a torch—flickers about over the curtain, and a voice speaks.*)

VOICE—All things are possible.

ANDREW *and* PAUL—Wh-what's that, wh-who's there?

VOICE—-Do not be afraid, I have come to grant your wish. We are going to venture out and meet some of your brothers, who are also members of the world-wide Brotherhood of Scouts. For this we must travel far and wide but, no matter where we go, we will find that we have brother Cubs everywhere, whether it be in Europe, America, Australia or Africa. Their uniforms and activities will depend on where they live, but they all promise to do their duty to God and to do their best. First we shall travel right to the other side of the world—AUSTRALIA.

(*Noise of rushing wind. Behind a lighted sheet, boys can be seen and heard singing an Australian song. Curtains open, two boys appear and start throwing a ball to each other.*)

PAUL—Gosh, short sleeves, but, of course, it is summer here now, isn't it?

VOICE—Yes, and it's warm enough all the year round in this part of Australia. Their summers are very hot, and their winters are just like our summers.

(*Australian boys put their ball down, and start making preparations for laying and lighting a fire.*)

PAUL—What are they doing now?

VOICE—Fire lighting. They also have this in their test. Cubs are taught to clear a wide area around the fire before they light it, so they won't start a bush fire which can cause much damage. Many people have been burnt to death in bush fires, for a bush fire when lit, blazes and spreads at a great rate, and in only a few minutes it is far too big for anyone to stop. It then rushes across the country, burning crops and forests, farms and the cattle. Backswoodsmen have to be very careful about their camp fires. In many parts of Australia there are very strict rules that everyone must follow before they are allowed to light fires out of doors. Every Cub here must know them and obey.

ANDREW—I see they also have to make a pot of tea.

VOICE—Yes, and here I am afraid we must leave them.

(*Curtains pull together.*)

Where would you like to venture next, any ideas?

ANDREW—How about going back nearer home and visiting our French brothers across the water?

VOICE—Right, hold tight—

(*Sounds of rushing wind and everything goes black. Lights go on, and six Cubs are sitting in a semi-circle in front of their screen, tying knots.*)

VOICE—In France, some Cubs, called *Les Louveteaux*, wear bright yellow shirts and brown trousers. They do not have Arrow Badges, Proficiency Badges or the Link Badge as we do, but I think they enjoy doing the same kind of things as you do. You see, they are practising knots in preparation for camping and expeditions into the countryside. Some Cub Packs in France have girls and boys as members.

ANDREW—Good gracious, I wouldn't want girls in my Pack.

VOICE—They have finished their knotting practice, and now they appear to be dressing-up. No doubt they are going to do some play-acting.

ANDREW—That one over there looks like a monk now. I wonder what they are going to do?

VOICE—I think I know. They are going to do some play-acting about an episode in the life of St. Francis. Yes, they are starting now.

(VOICE *explains the story as the French Cubs act.*)

VOICE—Once the people who lived in the little city of Gubbia were in great trouble, for they feared the huge grey wolf that lived on the hills. It would creep down into the town and steal the sheep and cattle that belonged to the farmers. The people were so afraid of the wolf that they hardly ever went out of their houses. One day, Brother Francis visited the city, and the people told him of their fear. Brother Francis was very sorry

for them, and said that he would go up into the hills to meet the wolf. At first the people would not let him go, for they loved him, but Brother Francis would not keep back, and when he set out the people of the city went with him to the gate and from there watched him climb up into the hills. Brother Francis did not have to go far. The great grey wolf rushed out to meet him. Brother Francis stood quite still, and motioned to the wolf to come hither. He said, 'I command you in the name of Christ not to hurt me or anyone else.' The wolf stopped in his tracks and looked up at him as if he were indeed listening to Brother Francis, who went on, 'I want to make peace between you and all those people whom you have hurt, so that you will no longer harm and frighten them, and they will no longer be afraid but forgive you. At these words, the wolf hung his head and tried to show that he understood and would do all that Brother Francis had asked of him. Brother Francis promised the wolf that the people of the city would give him all the food he needed. Then Brother Francis held out his hand and the wolf lifted up his great paw and laid it into the hand stretched out to him. Together they walked back down the hill and into the city. At first the people were very much afraid and hung back, but Brother Francis said, 'Be not afraid, all is well.' When the people saw that indeed the wolf was harmless, they crowded round and made him welcome. And here we must say goodbye to our French brothers and speed on to yet another country. Where to this time, Paul?

PAUL—Akela said that next month will be our Canadian month. Do you think we could go there?

VOICE—Certainly. Here we go . . .'

(*Sounds of an aeroplane, and everything goes dark. Canadian Cubs sitting at a table covering books and repairing torn pages.*)

ANDREW—What are they doing?

VOICE—Part of their tests are to make a dust-cover for a book and demonstrate how to open a new book. They also have to demonstrate how to make simple repairs to a cover or a binding of a book and repair torn pages.

ANDREW—We have a Book Reader's Badge and do some of these things.

VOICE—The Canadian Cubs, in between their tests and badge work, go in for skating and building snow houses, so for the time being the Cub cap is put away and out come these furry hoods. See, these Cubs are going out now. I think they are going to do some tracking.

PAUL—It's terribly cold. Do you think we could go somewhere a bit warmer?

VOICE—If you like.

ANDREW—Do you think we could go to Holland? Our Pack has a link with a Dutch Pack in the Hague, and I write to one of the Sixers.

VOICE—Right. Next stop HOLLAND.

(*Sound of some form of travel. A group of Dutch Cubs are sitting in front of their screen making preparation for playing Kim's game.*)

VOICE—These boys belong to the 96 Group Robin Hood Pack, your link in the Hague, Andrew. You see their uniform is the same as ours, only their badges are different. These are some of the boys who are in the Spotted Six.

ANDREW—Oh, yes, we don't have a Spotted Six in England.

VOICE—I'm not sure if there are any others in Holland. This is rather a stubborn idea of Akela de Rijke the Cub Leader. He felt that you can have brown, grey, black and white wolves, but never green, blue or yellow, so he put brown, grey and black triangles together and introduced a spotted Six. These boys are playing Kim's Game with some of their national paintings. They are very proud of their famous Dutch painters, and this is a good way of learning about the history and treasures of their own land.

ANDREW—Gosh, how interesting.

VOICE—As you know, Holland is a very small country with a dense population. This means that the western part of the country is becoming one large town, an ocean of houses and factories. It is impossible, therefore, for many Packs to have their own headquarters, and this Pack hold their Meetings in a basement of a large house. See, they have finished Kim's Game and they also are dressing-up.

PAUL—What *are* they going to do?

VOICE—Let us wait and see—ah, yes, they are going to do some play-acting about St. Nicolas.

ANDREW—St. Nicolas? Who is he?

VOICE—Well, you have heard of Santa Claus?

ANDREW—Of course.

VOICE—Well, these Cubs have already had their Christmas celebrations on 6th December, which is the birthday of 'Sint Nicolaas', as they call him. In winter it is people's festival number one.

(*If time is still needed for Cubs to get into their costumes, continue thus*:)

Where the theme comes from is not exactly clear. It is very old indeed, and appears even in the Middle Ages. There is a legend that long ago a Bishop visited his parishes, riding his horse. In one village he found that a cruel father had cut up his four children in pieces and put them in a barrel, salted the flesh, intending to eat them in due time. That Bishop, by the name of Nicolas (later he became a Saint), put the children together, took them with him on his white horse and did not forget to punish that cruel father, who, of course, said that he would not do it again.

That's why Saint Nicolas is the Patron of the children. Ah, they seem to be ready:

(*Cubs begin play-acting.*)

VOICE—Saint Nicolas, a Roman Catholic Bishop, came from Myra. In the month of November, he arrives with his white horse on a steamship from Spain. With him is his faithful servant, a Moor. There is always a crowd to watch and welcome him, that is bigger than when the Queen herself is visiting the town. That white horse is a very special horse, because it runs on the roofs of houses as easily as if it were on streets. That servant, called Black Peter (Zwarte Piet) is an acrobat,

so he has no difficulties in creeping through chimneys listening at most unbelievable places to hear if children have been obedient during the past year. On the evening before the 6th December, the children are allowed to put their shoe before the chimney, and in it they put a carrot or a slice of bread or a bit of hay for the horse; they also put a saucer of water beside it. St. Nicolas then sends his Black Peter to the house of each well-behaved child to strew candy and special small sugary figures as a kind of reward, and put some presents in the shoes. But the child who has no sweet, finds a small paper-bag of salt together with a rod (of willow branches) to be punished. Central heating systems don't give any difficulties.

ANDREW—That was all most interesting.

VOICE—I'm glad you enjoyed it. However, we must leave Holland now and make our last visit. This time we are going to the UNITED STATES OF AMERICA, where you will see some Cub Scouts. They only have a Pack Meeting once a month, but they meet in small groups, called Dens, once a week under the charge of a Den Mother. She is usually a parent of one of the boys. It is like a gang of your own friends, having lots of fun and games together. Then once a month these Dens of Cubs meet their Akela, when they have all their ceremonies and a very special Pack Meeting. Tonight we shall visit one of these Dens—

(*Sounds of rushing wind or travel—stage in darkness.*)

VOICE—See—the American flag, and all the Cub Scouts in this Den are standing round it. Let us listen for a while.

DEN MOTHER—Cubs, let us give the Pledge of Allegiance.

ALL CUBS—I pledge allegiance to the flag of the United States of America, and to the Republic for which it stands; one nation under God, indivisible, with liberty and justice for all.

DEN MOTHER—Tonight we have an initiation for a new Bobcat Cub Scout.

(*American Cubs form a semi-circle. One new Cub Scout goes and stands in front of the* DEN MOTHER.)

DEN MOTHER—Have you passed your Bobcat test with your parents?

NEW CUB SCOUT—Yes, I have.

DEN MOTHER—Tell us, what does the Cub Scout sign mean?

NEW CUB SCOUT—The Cub Scout sign means be quiet, pay attention. The two fingers are like the Wolf's ears, alert.

DEN MOTHER—What else does it mean?

NEW CUB SCOUT—It also means a Cub Scout is always obedient, and is fair, happy and game. He is square to himself and to others.

DEN MOTHER—Please will you give the Cub Scout Promise.

NEW CUB SCOUT—I. . . . . .promise

To do my best
To do my duty
To God and my Country
To help other people
and
to obey the Law of the Pack.

DEN MOTHER—Please give the Law of the Pack.

NEW CUB SCOUT—The Cub Scout follows Akela
The Cub Scout helps the Pack go
The Pack helps the Cub Scout grow
The Cub Scout gives good-will.

DEN MOTHER—'You have learned well the ways of the Bobcat. We welcome you to Den Number 1. (*She shakes hands with the* CUB SCOUT.)

ALL CUB SCOUTS—WELCOME BOBCAT. (*Shouted.*)

(*Stage blacks out.* ANDREW *and* PAUL *quickly resume their seats at the side of the stage. Lights come on and the two boys are seen rubbing their eyes and stretching.*) AKELA *comes on and calls*—PACK, PACK, PACK.

Investiture Ceremony—Foreign Cubs form background. (*This should not be a real ceremony, and the boy used in the demonstration should already have been invested.*)

(*Just before the Grand Howl—*)

AKELA—'Cubbing is part of family life throughout many countries around the world. In all of these free countries on an evening such as this, Cubs are joining in a Grand Howl, and repeating the Cub Scout Promise. Shall we in the. . . . . .Pack all renew our Cub Scout Promise.'

Grand Howl.

A DISTRICT PAGEANT WITH AN INTERNATIONAL THEME.

This would have the same introduction as the International Parents' Evening, with each country represented by a different Pack. (Individual rehearsals are all that is necessary.) The whole thing should take place in a large roped-off arena, with parents and friends all around. The introduction should be pre-recorded and relayed over a loudspeaker system with Sixer, new Cub and Scouter miming. The voice should be live. The entrance into the Arena should be wide enough to allow one Pack to run out whilst another is coming in. Ideas for countries and their displays are as follows:

MEXICO.

Rustlers.

Commentary by Voice:

Now, let us go and see what the Cubs of Mexico are up to . . . (*sound of travel*). Ah, yes, they are going to play a game called Rustlers. The boys are forming up in two teams,

facing one another. The four boys standing in the middle each have a rope. One team are Mexican drovers, the others Yankee drovers. The four boys are rustlers. At the words 'Forward Ho', the two teams of drovers will try to change places. The Rustlers will try to catch the drovers, and if they do, they must tie their rope round the drovers' ankles (hog-tie them). The hog-tied drovers then join the Rustlers in catching the other drovers.

AMERICA.

Commentary by Voice:

Let us visit the Cub Scouts of America. Hold tight, here we go . . . (*sound of travel*). They have to perform an Indian Dance for one of their tests—here they come now . . .

(*An Indian Dance is performed in costume with drums, etc.*)

JAPAN.

Commentary by Voice:

Next—Japan . . . (*sound of travel*). The art of folding paper is one of the first crafts learned by young children, and

Cubs are often taught it at their Pack Meetings. There are also many Festivals in Japan. We are now going to see Cubs in Japan in a holiday mood . . .

(*Cubs enter in Japanese costume with a variety of giant lanterns, fish, etc., held high on poles. Giant masks of*

K

many colours are held in front of Cubs as they all dance round the Arena to suitable music.)

HONG KONG.

Commentary by Voice:

Next, let us visit Hong Kong . . . (*sound of travel*). Here the Cubs are in holiday mood. Look, they are going to do a Dragon Dance . . .

(*A long line of Cubs underneath a 'dragon skin' perform a dance to suitable music.*)

AUSTRALIA.

Commentary by Voice:

Australia is our next stop . . . (*sound of travel*). Their activities and games are all very similar to our own. (*Cubs enter Arena.*) They are going to play a game called Cane Cutters' Relay. The rolled newspaper on each log represents a cane-knife. When their Akela calls 'Go', number one will run up to his log, grab the cane-knife and run back to his team where he will cut the cane (team has to jump over to avoid the knife). Then at the end of the team, number one turns and lops off the top of the cane. (*Cubs drop on hands and knees to avoid being hit on the head with the cane-knife.*) The cane-knife is then replaced on the log and number two repeats the performance.

(*Cubs play Cane Cutters' Relay.*)

VOICE—Here, I'm afraid, we must leave Australia and sail across the sea to New Zealand . . . (*sound of travel*).

(*Cubs enter in Maori costume.*)

Commentary by Voice:

See, they are dressed in Maori costume. Boys and girls all over New Zealand know how to play the stick game, and that is what we are going to see now.

(*Cubs perform Maori Stick Game.*)

Music and words are in *The Gilwell Camp Fire Book*, p. 73. Out of print, but probably available in your Group Library.

ITALY.

Commentary by Voice:

Now to the country of music and song—Italy . . . (*sound of travel*). Here we see the Cubs with home-made instruments making their own music.

(*Cubs enter and parade round the Arena making their own music.*)

AFRICA.

Commentary by Voice:

Let us now watch some Cub activities from Africa . . . (*sound of travel*). They will play a game from the Congo, called 'Hunting the Antelope'. One Cub is the Antelope, the rest are hunters. The hunters can only move about on all fours. In this position they move about within the area marked by Bamboos and try to trip the Antelope up. The Cub who is successful in doing this, then becomes the new Antelope.

(*Cubs play their game whilst the commentary is being given.*)

FRANCE.

Commentary by Voice:

Now, into France . . . (*sound of travel*). The Cubs, called *Louveteau*, wear bright yellow shirts and brown trousers. Here they come. (*Cubs enter the Arena.*) We are now going to see them doing some play-acting. One of their activities is to tell an episode in the life of St. Francis.

(*Use the same story as for International Parents' Evening.*)

SWEDEN.

Commentary by Voice:

Next, let us visit Sweden . . . (*sound of travel*). On the 30th April, large bonfires are built to welcome spring, but just as traditional as these is the dance around the decorated Midsummer pole at the end of June. (*Cubs enter the Arena.*) Look, here come the Cubs wearing folk costume. Now Swedish summer is at its most beautiful and in the north the midsummer sun is shining.

(*Cubs dance round the Midsummer Pole.*)

HOLLAND.

Commentary by Voice:

Our next stop—Holland . . . (*sound of travel*). Again we shall see Cubs dressed in costume, but this time they are playing a rather unusual game. Let me explain—(*Cubs enter and form up into two teams*). In the town of Alkmaar, a cheese market was held weekly. Each wholesaler had his own carriers, men dressed in white and wearing a special colour of hat. The cheeses were piled on wooden stretchers, and it was always a competition between the carriers to see who were the fastest couple without the cheeses falling off the stretcher.

(Cubs are dressed in white shirts, white trousers and wearing straw hats, one team with a blue band and the other with a red band round the crown. Each team has a wooden stretcher with a number of 'Edam' cheeses (small balloons

covered with papier-mache and painted red) piled up high. The teams race each other round the Arena, stopping to pick up any cheeses that might fall.)

IRELAND.

Commentary by Voice:

Now to Ireland . . . (*sound of travel*). See, the Irish Cubs are showing us the story of their Patron Saint—St. Patrick.

(*Enter Cubs in costume for play-acting. They mime the play as the Voice speaks.*)

There is the little shepherd boy, Patrick, watching his father's sheep. Oh, he has fallen asleep. What is happening over there? Pirates! They are capturing all the young boys in the neighbourhood. Now they have spotted Patrick, and he, too, is being taken prisoner. The pirates are taking their captives to Ireland—and now they are being sold as slaves to the local farmers.

After six years of looking after the swine, Patrick escaped, and went back to his home, but when his kinsmen begged him to remain with them he shook his head. He had work to do. He studied and studied, and became first a priest and then a bishop. And so he chose certain monks who had worked with him: they returned to Ireland, where they journeyed up and down the country preaching the Gospel. In the end the Irish heard him gladly and all loved him very much.

SWITZERLAND.

Commentary by Voice.

We must leave Ireland now, and make our last call. This time we are going to Switzerland . . . (*sound of travel*). Although this is only a small country in the heart of Europe, it has about 50,000 Scouts. Wherever one goes in Switzerland it is possible to see displays of flag-waving. (*Cubs enter, each with a large flag, a piece of coloured sheeting on a pole.*) Here come the Cubs to show you how it is done. (*Cubs form up into lines and do a display of flag-waving to music.*)

VOICE—I'm afraid our travels are over, so it is back to England.

(AKELA *comes on and calls*, 'PACK, PACK, PACK'. *Cubs of different countries run on and form a Parade Circle. The Investiture Ceremony takes place. This should not be a real ceremony, but only for demonstration.*)

AKELA—You are now a Cub Scout, and one of the world-wide Brotherhood of Scouts.

Cubbing is part of a family life in sixty countries around the world. In all of these free countries on an afternoon such as this, Cubs are repeating the Cub Promise and joining in the Grand Howl.

Shall we in....................District all renew our Cub Promise. Cubs alert.

ALL—I Promise that I will do my best
To do my duty to God, and to the Queen
To help other people
And to keep the Cub Scout Law.

(*Grand Howl by all Cubs.*)

(*Final march round the Arena to music.*)

GAMES

Egg Flip Relay.

Equipment needed: one egg-box per Six (each compartment numbered one to six)
two or three buttons per boy

Number clearly each compartment from one to six. Cubs form up in their Sixes behind a chalk-line, and each boy is given two or three buttons. An egg carton is then placed a yard or so in front of each Six. In relay fashion the Cubs try and throw their buttons into the carton. One throw per button. Highest score wins.

Noughts and Crosses Quiz.

Equipment needed: chalk or ropes
printed cards

This is an ideal game when Akela is single-handed, and groups for different Arrow requirements are out of the question.

Draw the following diagram on the floor in chalk, or use ropes and printed cards. Make out sets of large cards of O's and X's.

Flags and History	Knots	Health Rules
Water Safety	POT LUCK	First Aid
Discovering Nature	Feats of Skill	Home Safety

Divide the Pack into O's and X's. The first boy from 'O' team steps forward and chooses a square. Akela asks a question on whatever subject is chosen, and if it is answered correctly, an 'O' card is placed on the square, and the boy goes to the back of his team. If the wrong answer is given, it is offered to the first boy of 'X' team. First team to complete a line of X's or O's wins.

The Cubs will find this an extremely exciting game, and much learning and revision will be achieved. Set a time limit for each question or the game will lag.

Motor Relay. (A disguised form of 'Fishes in the Sea'.)

Equipment needed: one chair per boy

A semi-circle of boys sitting on chairs. Give each set of three or four boys a name of a car—Rolls Royce, Vauxhall, Ford, Datsun, etc. When the make of car is called, boys get up and run out of the opening and round the circle in a clockwise direction. A call of 'Join the M1' means change direction; 'steep hill', boys walk; 'foggy weather' means pigeon steps; 'crash up', boys run in through the gap and find a chair. (In the meantime a chair has been placed facing outwards.) When 'Crash up' is called, 'cars' must keep going, with no turning back allowed.

Money Bag.

Equipment needed: a bag of mixed coins per Six.

Each Six sits in a circle with the Sixer holding a bag of mixed coins. Akela in the centre of the room calls out 'five pence' and the Sixer has to put his hand into the bag and, without looking, find the correct coin. He then runs with it to Akela. First boy wins a point for his Six. Continue round each circle letting each boy take a turn with the bag.

Opposites.

Equipment needed: none

A good warming-up game that needs plenty of concentration by small boys is 'Opposites'. A number of orders are given fairly slowly at first and then quickened up, but the Cubs must do the exact opposite to every command.

Robin Hood and the Sheriff.

Equipment needed: two bean-bags or similar, to represent bags of gold

Two lines of boys, hands behind backs, turn inwards and face their opposite number. One line, Robin Hood and his Merry Men, and the other the Sheriff and his soldiers. Each leader has a bag of gold. Robin Hood begins by walking down the line behind his men. The idea is to give the bag to

one of them without the opposite number realising it. In order to mislead, Robin Hood can pretend to give the bag to several others. He then walks back to his place and shouts 'Go'. The one with the gold then runs up behind his own line, crosses over to the opposite side, down behind the soldiers, across the bottom and back to his place. At the same time his opposite number crosses over, through the gap and round clockwise, trying to catch him and capture the gold.

The merry men and soldiers take turns in capturing the other's gold. Chalk up the score of bags of gold.

Penny Faces.

Equipment needed: one sheet of paper per Six

Trace round a penny a dozen times on a large sheet of paper, and draw the same eyes and nose on each penny face. Give a copy to each Six and ask them to produce 12 portraits by adding the remaining features.

Winter Store.

Equipment needed: five objects to represent nuts per Cub
chalk

Each Cub is a squirrel, and stands beside his store cupboard (a chalk circle), inside which are five 'nuts'. When Akela calls 'Go' each squirrel has to keep grabbing one nut at a time from his neighbours' stores to add to his own. When Akela calls 'stop', each squirrel counts his nuts. If you have a large Pack in a small room, have boys sitting-out to cheer on the others. After each go, any squirrel with no nuts falls out and others take his place.

Lay the Table.

Equipment needed: none

A game rather like Port and Starboard. The call of 'knife' means stand still, arms at sides.

Fork—stand still, arms held high.
Spoon—crouch as for Grand Howl.
Lay the table—lie flat on the floor.
Clear the cloth—run to sides of room.
Salt—run to the top of the room.
Pepper—run to the bottom of the room.

Telegrams.

Equipment needed: slips of paper (telegrams)

Write out various telegrams on slips of paper. On the word 'Go', Sixers run up, look at the first telegram and run back to their Six and whisper the message to the next boy who in turn passes the message on. The last boy calls out the message. Boys should take it in turn to run up and memorise the telegram.

Setting-up Camp Relay.

Equipment needed: playing-cards
chalk

Six yards or so in front of each Six, draw a chalk circle. Give each boy two playing-cards, and on the word 'Go', number one runs up and erects his 'Tent', then goes back and touches off the next boy, etc. If one boy flattens another's 'tent' he must erect this as well as his own before running back to his Six.

Crab Race.

Equipment needed: one rope per Six

Sixes in lines. Give the Sixer a rope, and on the word 'Go', Six stand back-to-back with each other. The Sixer ties them together and they set off to the other end of the room. *Do make sure that the rope is tied round their waists and held there.*

'Whack'ems.'

Equipment needed: a stocking filled loosely with rags

A favourite game with Cubs is 'Whack'ems', but how too often do we have to hunt around for something to do the whacking? A stocking filled loosely with rags makes an ideal, and not too hard, 'whacker'.

Cubs form a circle and put their hands behind their backs. One Cub with the stocking, walks round and then places the stocking in a Cub's hand. That boy then turns and chases the Cub on his right round the circle and back to his place, all the time trying to whack him on the seat of his trousers.

Skipping Marathon.

Equipment needed: one large rope.

With two Scouters turning the rope, each Six in turn runs in and skips while the rest of the Pack count out loud. Six with the highest number of skips is the winner. This game helps the boy who finds skipping difficult, enabling him to get the correct rhythm and gain confidence.

Teeth Drawing.

Equipment needed: paper and pencil per Cub

Sit the Cubs round a table with a pencil and paper and tell them to hold their pencil between their teeth and draw an animal picture. No hands allowed.

Battle of Snakes.

Equipment needed: none

Two lines of Cubs, each holding the waist of the boy in front. On the word 'Go', the head of each snake tries to touch the tail of the other snake. If the tail is caught, it becomes the head of the other snake. If any boy lets go and breaks his line, he and all the boys behind him join the end of the other snake. Continue until only one snake is left.

Wig Makers.

Equipment needed: old magazines
paper and pencils

Cut out various faces from magazines, but make sure that you cut off all the hair. Mount these faces on sheets of white paper and ask the Cubs to draw the hair to fit the face. Felt tip pens might be better than pencils.

Fishing.

No doubt many Scouters still have a great many of the old-type clothes-peg, so why not use them for a fishing-game? Put a bunch of numbered clothes-pegs in a tub of water, and give each boy a fishing-rod. This is just a piece of string tied

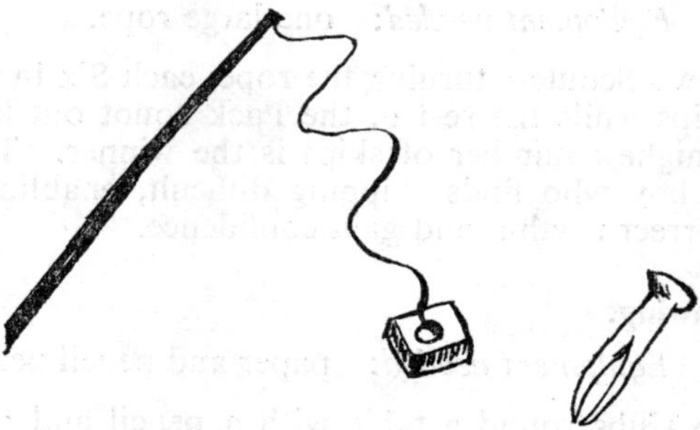

to a stick, with a nut tied to the free end of the string. The idea is to get the nut between the slot of the clothes-peg and lift it out of the water. Highest score wins.

Toothbrush and the Germ.

Equipment needed: none

It has been seen from recent newspaper reports that children's teeth are sadly neglected. We should, therefore, take every opportunity of letting our boys know how important it is to look after their teeth. The game **Toothbrush and the Germ** makes them think on the right lines, and at the same time provides enormous fun.

A circle of boys holding hands represent teeth. One boy in the centre is the germ, and another, on the outside, the toothbrush. The teeth try to stop the toothbrush reaching the germ. Should the toothbrush break through the teeth, the germ must be quickly let through the teeth, and so on until the germ is caught. Give each pair of boys two or three minutes. Should the germ not be caught in the given time, tell the boys that that particular toothbrush needs renewing.

Dictionary Relay—Book Reader Badge.

Equipment needed: one dictionary per Six (large print)

The Cubs are numbered in Six lines with one dictionary per Six. Call out a word and number. The first boy to find the word reads out the meaning. Remember to call out easy words of three or four letters, otherwise the game will become boring to the boys awaiting their turn.

Kim's Game.

(*a*) Pin a large colourful poster on the wall, and let the Cubs study it for two minutes. Cover the picture and ask a dozen already prepared questions about it. Sixers write down the answers helped by the Six.

(*b*) Using a cassette recorder, record sounds in certain categories, i.e. sounds in the home, seashore, railway station, a busy market, etc.

(*c*) Two Scouters stand, one on either side of a doorway or curtains. Objects are thrown from one person to another. The Cubs watch and then try to write out a list of what they saw.